THE CHARACTER OF A CHRISTIAN LEADER

THE CHARACTER OF A CHRISTIAN LEADER

originally titled
The Six Wings of the Seraph

by St. Bonaventure

translated by Philip O'Mara

SERVANT BOOKS
ANN ARBOR, MICHIGAN

copyright © 1978 by Servant Books

Published by:
Servant Books
P.O. Box 8617
Ann Arbor, Michigan 48107

Available from:
Servant Books
Distribution Center
237 N. Michigan
South Bend, Indiana 46601

ISBN 089283-044-1

Printed in the United States of America

Contents

INTRODUCTION

The Character of a Christian Leader is, as far as I can tell, unique in all of Christian literature. Bonaventure wrote the treatise, originally titled *The Six Wings of the Seraph*, in the thirteenth century. His purpose was to instruct heads of religious communities. Many documents have been written to set forth a rule of life for a community—the *Longer Rules* of St. Basil and *The Rule of St. Benedict* are but two examples—but Bonaventure alone has written about how to get the community to live up to its ideal.

To understand Bonaventure's instructions, we must bear in mind that he was writing for men charged with *governing* a Christian community. This is a concept of pastoral leadership with which we may be unfamiliar. Bonaventure was not talking about guidance for the interior spiritual life, still less about psychological counselling. Nor did he emphasize purely managerial or organizational aspects of leadership. Instead, he was concerned with the type of service that consists of providing a community and its members with authoritative direction.

Throughout Christian history, people seeking a more complete commitment to the Lord have often formed communities with a well-defined pattern of life, worship, and service. In such communities, the leaders exercise a greater degree of personal authority over both the group as a whole and the individual members. The leaders have a governmental function in establishing the pattern of life for the group; in teaching, counseling, forming, and correcting the members; and in directing and caring for the community and its individual members.

Pastoral leaders of our day may see little need for a book on community government. We teach, counsel, preach, preside, and so on, but seldom are we put in a position where we must govern. Nevertheless, I think that every Christian leader will benefit from careful study of the wisdom contained in this book.

Those who will benefit most are leaders who are responsible for exercising authority over the lives of other Christians in a particular group. This category would include pastors of community churches or fellowships, heads of covenant communities, superiors of religious orders, and heads of discipleship groups. Their positions are equivalent to those of the men Bonaventure was instructing in the thirteenth century.

These leaders will find value in both Bonaventure's practical wisdom and his emphasis on the essential characteristics of Christian leadership. After a brief opening chapter on the need for authority and the type of men who should be heads, Bonaventure devotes his treatise to the six virtues most needed by a Christian leader: zeal for righteousness, brotherly love, patience, an exemplary life, discretion, and devotion to God. Bonaventure compares each quality to one wing of a seraph (see Isa. 6:2), hence the original name of the book. Such metaphors were a common medieval device for structuring.

As Bonaventure describes these six qualities, he deals with many practical questions that face the leader of a community: What are my duties as head? How strict should I be with members of the community? When should I correct? When forbear? How should the members regard me and my authority? How can I help weaker members of the community? What do I do when the community is divided or when some members oppose me? How can I care for the administration of the community as well as its spiritual life?

Christian leaders in situations other than communities will also benefit from *The Character of a Christian Leader*. Bonaventure's definition of the six virtues needed for Christian leadership have universal value. Readers will also discover that much of his advice about behavior and relationships applies to all in pastoral service. Consider, for example, his advice on patience (pp. 25-32). What pastor would not be the better for learning how to inspire confidence in the weak and soothe the angry? And all pastoral leaders can improve their service by adopting Bonaventure's principles for distinguishing between administrative and spiritual duties (pp. 51-52).

Heads of families will also find this book helpful. Their responsibilities for governing, directing, and forming their children make their role analagous to that of the community head. Indeed, the New Testament itself makes the family the proving ground for Christian leaders (see 1 Tim. 3:4). How can a father get his children to follow the Lord? How should he train and correct three very different children? What standards should he use? Should he be strict or lenient? These are all points on which Bonaventure's insights will prove valuable.

Some familiarity with Bonaventure's history will aid readers in understanding his advice. Few facts about his youth have been preserved. He was born in Italy in the year 1221. We know that his name was Giovanni di Fidanza, but we do not know how he came to be called

Bonaventure. At some point between 1238 and 1243, he joined the Order of Friars Minor, commonly called the Franciscans.

The Friars Minor were still strongly marked by the character of their founder, Francis of Assisi, who had died in 1226. As a young man, Francis felt the Lord directing him to embrace absolute poverty and preach repentance, brotherly love, and peace. Accordingly, he renounced all property, literally refusing to come into direct contact with money. He supplied his needs by begging, and devoted himself to prayer and preaching. His example and simple joy proved infectious, generating one of the greatest renewal movements in the history of Christianity. By the time Bonaventure joined the Friars Minor, only thirty years after their founding, the order already numbered thousands of men.

Bonaventure was sent from the Roman province of the Franciscans to study at the University of Paris. There he earned renown as a great theologian and philosopher. He was a contemporary of Thomas Aquinas, and many scholars regard him as Aquinas' equal in ability and achievement.

In 1257, the year he was recognized as a doctor of philosophy, Bonaventure was elected minister general of his order. He set aside his studies, and for the next seventeen years served as head of the Franciscans. His contributions to the order during those years were so significant that he is often called its second founder.

One of Bonaventure's first tasks as minister general was to heal a serious rift that had opened over the interpretation of Francis's rule of life, particularly as it involved poverty. One party of monks favored a literal observance of the absolute poverty practiced by Francis; another allowed for modification. Bonaventure dealt firmly with the extreme elements on both sides of the controversy. He disciplined some members of the stricter party who had adopted heretical ideas, but at the same time he initiated a reform of the order that resulted in a stricter interpretation of the rule. In other words, he refused to side with either faction, but saw what was good on each side and sought to make that the rallying point for unity.

Later in his life, Bonaventure was often called to serve the larger church as well as the Franciscans. In 1271, he was asked to moderate a dispute over the papal election. He declined an archbishopric offered in 1265, but was eventually made a cardinal. The final significant event of his life was his involvement in the Fourteenth Ecumenical Council in 1274 at Lyons, France, where he was instrumental in attempts to reunite the Greek and Roman churches. He died unexpectedly during the council, on July 15, 1274.

Despite his high position and great prestige, Bonaventure always remained personally involved in the lives of his brothers. He usually performed the regular visitations to various Franciscan houses himself, rather than appoint others to take his place. A typical example of his concern is the story told of a brother at one friary who wanted to talk with Bonaventure, but was too shy to do so. By the time the brother finally got up his courage to speak, Bonaventure had completed his visit and was back on the road. Determined not to lose his opportunity altogether, the brother managed to catch up with the travellers and had a lengthy conversation with Bonaventure.

The brother headed back home greatly strengthened, but some of Bonaventure's companions were impatient with the delay. Bonaventure responded to them as a true pastor:

"My brethren," he said, "I could not do otherwise. I am at the same time both prelate and servant, and that poor brother is both my brother and my master. These are the words of the rule: 'The ministers shall receive the brethren with charity and kindness, and so hold themselves towards them that the brethren shall be able to treat with them as masters with their servants, for the ministers must be the servants of all the friars.' And so I, as minister and servant, must be at the disposal of this poor brother who is my master, and help him according to my ability and his needs."[1]

This, then, was the spirit of our author. Bonaventure belongs to the ancient line of great Christian pastors which extends back to Benedict, Basil the Great, and Bernard of Clairvaux. Like his great predecessors, he was concerned to lead men to God, to form them for a life devoted to God, and to teach them to serve God faithfully as part of a community of men dedicated to the same goals.

It would be well for the reader to keep Bonaventure's history in mind, for some of his advice is directed to the particular conditions he faced, conditions that have since changed. For example, the controversy he faced within the Franciscans led him to warn community heads to expect intense opposition from those in their charge. Heads of communities ought not be surprised by opposition from members, and they will surely find Bonaventure's advice helpful should such opposition arise. But it is not likely that they will encounter divisions as severe as those in the early Franciscans.

Another example is the particular type of obedience that Bonaventure presumed members owed to their heads. The members of the Friars Minor vowed complete obedience to their superiors, but few community heads nowadays are in the same position. Even many religious orders, though still maintaining the formal

---

[1]*Butler's Lives of the Saints*, edited, revised, and supplemented by Herbert Thurston, S.J., and Donald Attwater, Volume III (New York: P.J. Kenedy and Sons, 1956) p. 99.

vow of obedience, now interpret it quite differently. People today often dislike the idea of true headship and obedience because they have had experience with a system which was not working properly. We should, however, understand that this type of authority has been successfully used in many Christian communities in the past, and not allow our modern apprehension to prevent us from understanding Bonaventure.

Bonaventure's stance on punishment is also typical of his times. Civil and ecclesiastical tribunes in the middle ages meted out severe physical punishments, and physical discipline was also common in monastic communities as far back as the fifth century. This accounts for Bonaventure's discussion of punishment. With the exception of its role in childrearing, however, punishment as presented by Bonaventure is not part of modern Christian community life.

Some of Bonaventure's advice would actually be inappropriate for leaders in today's conditions. For example, he urges the head of the community to be loved more than feared, advice that balanced the authoritarian tendencies of his own time. In every age, Christian leaders must heed the Master's directions not to lord it over those under them (see Mark 10:41-45). However, the temper of our times is such that many Christian leaders are overly concerned with receiving approval from those they serve. They shy away from firm stands on important issues for fear their subordinates will reject them. In such cases, Bonaventure's advice must be tempered with an emphasis on the need for firmness and aggressiveness in exercising authority.

Bonaventure's recommendation of constant self-scrutiny might also be inappropriate for today's leaders. Our modern environment encourages excessive introspection. Never before in history, it seems to me, have so many people turned in on themselves. This preoccupation with our emotions paralyzes many Christians, so that they are unable to perform even minimal service to others. Given this unhealthy inclination, Christian leaders would do well to modify Bonaventure's advice on self-examination. We ought to encourage those in our care to assess themselves with sober judgment, but instruct them to avoid some of the popular forms of self-analysis.

Philip O'Mara has produced an excellent version of Bonaventure's treatise. He has made the text more readable by simplifying the author's reliance on the six wings metaphor, and he has chosen English terms designed to help modern readers better understand Bonaventure's thought. For example, he has translated "religious order" as "community." He has also adopted the terms "head" or "leader" to translate Bonaventure's Latin terms for the one in charge of the community; these terms are not exact equivalents, but they seemed best suited to the author's meaning.

Dr. O'Mara also made every effort to produce an ecumenically sensitive text. However, Bonaventure did write within a thoroughly Roman Catholic context, and it was necessary to preserve that context in order to be faithful to the author. Thus, the divine office, canon law, pontiffs, and monasteries are all occasionally discussed in the book. Protestant readers should note that Bonaventure's discussion of these forms need not prevent them from receiving his excellent advice on community government.

Bert Ghezzi

THE
CHARACTER
OF A
CHRISTIAN LEADER

PROLOGUE

Give instruction to a wise man, and he will be still   Prov. 9:9
wiser. A wise man takes advantage of his opportunities.
He finds something to deepen his wisdom in the least
important occasion; even another person's dullness
will often help him become more perceptive.

This essay has been written for heads of Christian
communities who are new to their responsibilities and
for those who will soon take on such tasks. It aims to
give them a chance to devote more thought to the pre-
cise discernment of good and evil. Much of our attention will be given to various errors, but the goal of this
discussion is to teach heads to be diligent in calling
their communities on to more spiritual and service-
oriented conduct.

A person who commits himself to life in a Christian
community and accepts a call to serve within it as the
head needs to study the many topics treated in this
book, and more besides. Men of real wisdom, after all,
have been willing to study the behavior of brute animals, in order to find ideas that would apply to their
own arts and skills.

CHAPTER ONE

THE NEED FOR CHRISTIAN LEADERS

1. *I am writing these instructions to you so that . . . you may know how one ought to behave in the household of God, which is the church of the living God.* Paul wrote twice to Timothy, whom he had made bishop of the church at Ephesus, to teach him how to act in exercising the authority committed to him. Timothy had already learned to live a holy life as an individual Christian; now Paul wanted to teach him how to exercise authority over other Christians in a way that would be useful to them and meritorious in him. For while living peacefully among equals and submitting humbly to authority call for certain abilities in a man, providing useful headship demands others.

    Bernard of Clairvaux writes, "Understand this: many men live quietly enough under the personal rule of another, but if you remove that yoke, prove unable to be quiet any longer—unable to keep themselves from any kind of wrongdoing. Furthermore, you find that certain men live, to the best of their ability, in peace with everyone, and hardly need a master at all; yet they are not suited to headship themselves. *According to the measure of faith which God has assigned* they are content with a kind of good mediocrity. They know how to live with the members of the community in peace and harmony. But once they are placed over their brethren, their leadership is useless, foolish and harmful. Those who know how to serve as heads are better, therefore, than the other two kinds of people."[1]

Exod. 18:21-22

For this reason Moses was instructed not to put just anyone in charge of the people, but to choose out of the entire people those men who were expert and capable of serving as judges. Someone who accepts responsibility for making others good should have already learned the self-discipline necessary for goodness, so that his Christian virtue has become habitual through constant

Acts 1:1

practice. *Jesus began to do and teach:* the Lord is presented as first doing the things he later taught.

Why Have Leaders?

Heb. 5:12

2. Beginners in the Christian life need a head so that they can be taught what they do not know: *You need someone to teach you . . . the first principles of God's word.* There is much that they must learn for the sake of their own salvation and spiritual progress—what to avoid; what to take pleasure in; what to do, hope for, fear; how to tell the lesser from the greater evils, and the good from the better.

Furthermore, it is not enough only to know what is good. A Christian must also be trained to practice these virtues. A medical student is expected to study his material and then develop his skill by working with the sick, because practice imprints knowledge on the mind more effectively than study alone. This applies to the skills of every discipline. Yet often those who have not mastered their trade are reluctant to take the trouble to improve their skills. They need at times to have someone who will insist that they practice.

The heads of a Christian community are therefore accustomed to exercise the people in their care in various virtues that they need to acquire, such as humility,

[1]Sermons on The Song of Songs, 23, n.8

brotherly love, patience, obedience, sexual morality, devotion, sobriety, silence, and others. Those committed to the Christian life should be led to practice these virtues and to overcome the vices opposed to them: *Bring them up in the discipline and instruction of the Lord.* The more our virtue advances, the more our vices grow weak.   *Eph. 6:4*

Beginners in Christian life must also be guided, so that they will not be dragged into sin, or for that matter, into imprudent practices of virtue. The fact is that the spiritually immature, those not yet cleansed from the effects of sin, are often held back from sin more by fear of man than fear of God. It is to their advantage to be under the direction of a head who can pull them out of danger, like a mother who protects her children from drowning or falling prey to wild animals. *For wisdom will come into your heart, and knowledge will be pleasant to your soul; discretion will watch over you; understanding will guard you; delivering you from the way of evil, from men of perverted speech.*   *Prov. 2:10-12*

Finally, a head should devote himself to correcting beginners in the spiritual life, because the force of sin is still alive in them to drag them down to a lower standard of conduct, just as a fever pushes a sick person into more serious illness, or a neglected wound becomes infected. The more involved one has been in a fault, the harder it is to rub out the stain by one's own power. One needs the help of a stronger person.

That is why God has willed that more mature Christians should have authority over beginners. In this way, if the beginners fall into sin or any neglectful or reckless conduct, the more mature can turn them back to righteousness, through their warnings, penalties, corrections and demands. The less mature, left to their own judgment, may well fail to see anything wrong in their bad conduct. Indifferent to their guilt, they will wallow in it longer and sink more deeply. Therefore they must humbly accept their head's direction, for a sick man cannot be healed unless he obeys the doctor.

Sinful passions are the infirmities characteristic of the human condition. Christ has given the leaders of his people the right to act on behalf of the weaker brethren *Jude 22* and to overcome what troubles them: *Convince some,* *Luke 9:1* *who doubt.* And, *he gave them power and authority over all demons and to cure diseases.*

Who Does Not Need a Director?

3. Those who wish to live without a head should be so enlightened by knowledge that they are never mistaken about anything that they need to know. They should be divinely qualified to discern spirits, so that no man or demon or impression of their own can ever *Phil. 4:12* deceive them as to what is good: *In any and all cir-circumstances I have learned the secret of facing* [my condition].

Such persons should also be so filled with devout fervor that they faithfully commit themselves, without urging from anyone else, to the best possible expres-*Phil. 3:13-14* sion of every virtuous practice: *Forgetting what lies behind and straining forward to what lies ahead, I press on.*

Again, they should be so inclined to love what is good that they find horror in everything evil. They must carefully abstain from anything that could give scandal *1 Cor. 10:32* and treat all people inoffensively and peaceably: *Give no offense to Jews or to Greeks.*

Next, they should be so humble that they are not puffed up by their own goodness, nor presume to lack all evils. In other words, they can judge precisely all their faults of thought, word and omission, and then amend themselves through strict correction.

Finally, they should be so steady in all these virtues that no trifle or distraction, to say nothing of genuine

difficulty or fear, can change their position: *Who shall*   *Rom. 8:35*
separate us from the love of Christ?

It is difficult to practice such virtues as these, and so there are few suited to life without submission to a head. For the same reason, those who direct others to a better and wiser life must themselves be subject to headship, right on up to the Sovereign Pontiff, who, as vicar of Christ, is the head of the whole Church militant.

4. Those who should exercise headship need to have different virtues. They need certain virtues in order to conduct their own lives without reproach, others to obey their own heads humbly, and still others to give worthwhile direction to the people in their care, calling them on to better things. A person responsible for teaching others how to practice the virtues ought to possess them all in the highest degree. For practical purposes, however, one can reduce the qualities needed in a superior or head to six that are especially important. They are like the six wings of the seraphim,   *Isa. 6:2* the angels who are the vanguard of the heavenly host; these wings are a means of both action and defense.

CHAPTER TWO

ZEAL FOR RIGHTEOUSNESS

1. The first characteristic that the head of a community needs is zeal for righteousness, so that his heart is troubled whenever he finds anything unjust in himself or in others. We judge a person's goodness by the extent to which he feels a pure and growing hatred for evil; for to the extent that we love something, we grieve at its destruction. Consequently we are accustomed to call four kinds of religious people "good."

2. The first are those who do no evil, yet do not devote themselves faithfully to doing good. They live with other people quietly and peaceably, offending no one and giving no scandal: *These men were very good to us and we suffered no harm.* We usually call such individuals good if their manners are inoffensive and they conduct themselves sociably with everyone, even though they seem to lack other, more positive virtues. In the same way we speak of baptized infants as good.

1 Sam. 25:15

3. There is a second, better group, who both refrain from evil and devote themselves to frequent good deeds. They understand how good it is to be sober, chaste, humble, loving toward their neighbors and faithful to prayer, and to practice the other virtues. But it is also characteristic of this group that while they do not neglect to do what good they can, they see no need to do more than that. They do not burn with desire for a

more complete holiness. So much prayer and fasting, so much keeping watch and working, so much alms giving: this is enough for them. They remain quietly content with this spiritual level, and abandon higher things to others. *So I saw that there is nothing better than that a man should enjoy his work; for that is his lot.*

Eccles. 3:22

4. Better still is the third group. They too detest and avoid wrongdoing, and fervently commit themselves to whatever good they can do. But when they have done all they can, they consider it nothing compared with what they long to do. Knowing that *while bodily training is of some value, godliness is of value in every way,* they eagerly desire the spiritual and internal virtues—fondness for prayer, an intimate knowledge of God, and the experience of divine love. They believe that they are nothing and have nothing, that they obtain no comfort from earthly or heavenly things, as long as they lack opportunity to exercise these virtues and enjoy the sweetness of devotion.

Luke 17:10
1 Tim. 4:8

This third group is not, however, inflamed with fervent zeal against the vices of others or the dangers of their sins. They want everyone to be good and live in grace, but feel no wound of sorrow when they see the opposite. They simply remain themselves intent upon God. When such men are called to direct others, they prove little suited to the task, because they put off caring for their charges in order to preserve their own peace. *Shall I leave my sweetness and my good fruit, and go to sway over the other trees?*

Judg. 9:11

5. The best persons for headship are those who avoid wrongdoing and practice virtue, but are also afire with zeal for righteousness and for souls. They obtain no comfort from progress toward their own salvation unless they are also leading others to God. The Lord is their example; although he always had complete joy in himself, he was not content only to possess glory, but *emptied himself, taking the form of a servant,* in order

Phil. 2:7

to lead many sons into glory with him through his
teaching and his work.

Zeal for righteousness, like *scarlet twice dyed,*[1]   *Exod.*
shines with the double glow of charity—love of God   *26:1,31,36*
and of neighbor. A person who loves God not only
desires to enjoy his goodness and be close to him, but
loves to see his will accomplished, his worship carried
out and his honor exalted. He wants all people to know,
love, serve, and honor God more than everything else.
A person who loves his neighbor desires not only
health and prosperity for him, but, even more, eternal
salvation. The more complete this charity becomes, the
more fervently do we desire to help people be saved,
the more determined is our eagerness for them, and the
purer our joy when they find salvation. For charity *does*   *1 Cor. 13:5*
not insist on its own way but seeks what is of God.

Love God and seek the things of God single-heart-
edly, and you will grieve to see him dishonored and
unknown, neither loved nor obeyed, his worship destroyed, his adversaries multiplied and rejoicing. To
the extent that you love your neighbor's salvation, you
will mourn his damnation and indeed anything harmful
to him.

Righteousness

6. Although all who are God's friends have to love
their neighbor too, brotherly love is especially necessary in those who are heads. Their position demands
that they act on God's behalf, and so their hearts should
be as much moved by love of righteousness and hatred
of wickedness, as is God's heart. *You love righteous-*   *Ps. 45:7*
ness and hate wickedness; therefore God, your God,
has anointed you. "Righteousness" here refers to all
the qualities needed for the salvation or spiritual progress of souls.

[1]Translated from the Vulgate.

7. In some cases the need for these qualities derives from eternal law; without humility, purity, love, mercy, and the like, no one is ever saved. The commandments of God, according to both the old and the new law, are especially directed toward these virtues: *You shall love* *the Lord your God with all your heart, and with all* *your soul, and with all your mind ... you shall love* *your neighbor as yourself. On these two command-* *ments depend all the law and the prophets.*

Matt. *22:37-40*

The need for some other qualities derives from human decrees, made on God's behalf by the authority of the Church, and canonically established for the benefit of all. The ritual to be observed in celebrating the sacraments is a good example. Canon law says that "the decrees of the canons ought to be observed by all," whether laymen or clergy, wherever the decrees apply to their situation.

Some requirements are demanded of people through their own free act; if a person, without being under any undue influence, willingly makes a vow, the law of God demands that he keep it. Thus, whatever the rule of a religious order imposes, such as obedience, giving up all one's wealth, and remaining celibate, the members of the order are obliged to live up to it. *When you make* *a vow to the Lord your God, you shall not be slack to* *pay it; for the Lord your God will surely require it of* *you, and it would be sin in you. But if you refrain from* *vowing, it shall be no sin in you. You shall be careful to* *perform what has passed your lips, for you have volun-* *tarily vowed to the Lord your God what you have* *promised with your mouth.*

Deut. *23:21-23*

Other qualities that go into righteousness have to do with the circumstances or situations in which we can make spiritual progress, although they do not refer to things necessary for salvation. Thus, there are rules about public worship and other prayers, about silence, work, food and clothing, keeping vigil and other spiritual exercises, which vary from one Christian community to another, according to what each group sees as helpful. Such exercises do not, in themselves, lead to salvation, nor does one lose one's salvation by breaking the rules concerning them. But breaking these rules does disrupt the good order of one's community, and so interferes with one's own spiritual progress and with the example which one ought to give others. A person who loves righteousness will be glad to see rules of this kind faithfully kept, and will encourage it, while it will grieve and anger him to see them broken. *Do I not hate them that hate thee, O Lord? And do I not loathe them that rise against thee?* Ps. 139:21

Judging Wrongdoing

8. A head's ability to judge right and wrong will increase as he deepens his awareness of serious wrongdoing and pays less attention to minor offenses. A wise man weighs all things as to their being good or bad, but a foolish man often regards serious matters as though they were trivial, and trivial as serious. To him a *speck* is like *a log;* he has *neglected weightier matters . . . straining out a gnat and swallowing a fly.* Such men are led, not by the Spirit of God, but by their own individual eagerness. For example, some heads of communities are very fervent in correcting a single failure to bow one's head at the right moment during common prayers, but they ignore the person who regularly gossips about the faults of another member of the community. They become more harshly indignant at the neglect of a minor ritual during prayers than at a serious and scandalous disturbance in the community. Matt. 7:3 Matt. 23:23-24

9. The most serious forms of wrongdoing, those which we should be most careful to avoid, are those that break any commandment of God or of the Church; those that violate any serious agreement a person has

voluntarily made, like observance of the rule of a religious order; and those that are likely to scandalize others by giving some appearance of evil. Signs of greed, pride, envy, gluttony, anger, disobedience, overly-intimate friendships, and other vices, give

Rom. 2:24 Christian communities a foul reputation. *The name of God is blasphemed among the gentiles because of you.*

People should be built up in faith by committed participants in Christian communities; they should learn from us what to do and what to avoid. They ought not to receive scandal from us, but be nourished in spirit by our good example. Even a gravely sinful action committed in secret is more easily cured than a scandal, for it may be healed by secret penance. But the effect of a scandal can hardly be extracted from the hearts of all who may have heard of it.

10. The second most serious type of wrongdoing is anything that interferes with fervent devotion. True faithfulness to religion derives from devotion, and every exercise of virtue is made fruitful by it. Religious commitment not anointed with this oil is arid. An organization devoted to good works is as unstable as a

Ezek. stone wall built without mortar when its participants
13:10-15 are not joined together through frequent and fervent
Matt. prayer. The lamps of the foolish virgins went out with-
25:1-13 out oil. In every Christian community where fervor grows tepid, actions that require other virtues begin to decline, and the community is in danger of ruin.

11. Finally, one must beware of neglecting exterior discipline, because that is a sign of a neglected conscience and interior superficiality. Rules of conduct are established to preserve the community's good order and to stabilize the spiritual progress of its members. Observance of such discipline, however, is not commanded on the grounds that it is wrong to live in any other way. Rather, it is better suited to the character of a community for the conduct of the brethren to conform

to a single pattern; if each member lives as he wishes and does as he pleases, he may disturb many others.

In all the details of exterior discipline, where a rule exists not to prevent evil but to support the goodness of the life of the community, a head must see to it that the rule is kept in the right spirit, faithfully but without scrupulous worry over every possible transgression. Otherwise, a custom that was originally good may give birth to a deformity, and concealment may nourish neglect. This does not mean that zeal for discipline should relax, but it should be forewarned against such evil consequences.

How to Deal with Wrongdoing

12. A head who has genuine zeal for righteousness will first of all not do or teach anything evil. Secondly, he will not permit evil in his community nor concede that it is acceptable, no matter what trickery or determination is used to sway him. Third, he will never encourage evil or show pleasure in it on occasions when it has actually been done behind his back. Fourth, he will not remain silent and pretend to know nothing when he ought to speak out, show how wrong an action is, and take precautions to prevent anyone from trying to do such a thing again. Finally, he will not let bad behavior go unpunished, for the punishment of sin brings about something good. Punishment keeps an individual from falling into further sin: *Sin no more,* *John 5:14* *that nothing worse befall you.* It cleanses the guilty person from a sin that God might otherwise punish more harshly: *If you beat him with a rod, you will save* *Prov. 23:14* *his life from Sheol.* And the punishment teaches others to avoid similar offenses: *Strike a scoffer, and the sim-* *Prov. 19:25* *ple will learn prudence.* Furthermore, the head himself, as a representative of our heavenly Judge, rescues himself from the sin of neglect by doing his duty. When

1 Sam.
4:11ff the priest Eli did not do this, he brought death on himself and his two sinful sons.

13. The difference between praiseworthy Christian communities and those that have lost their fervor is not that the praiseworthy ones have no sinful members, but that in them no one is allowed to misbehave without penalty. The gates to wrongdoing are carefully kept shut, and those who do good are shown favor and love, so that they persevere and improve continually. Even the community of the angels, before they were confirmed in grace, and the apostles, with Christ as their leader, *he charges with error.* What earthly body of good people would dare to claim the privilege of sinlessness for themselves? *You are clean but not all;* although many, through God's grace, are clear of sin, not all are.

Job 4:18

John 13:10

14. In fact, the mixture of good people and bad that is found in Christian communities is beneficial. For as long as the good members are still able to practice virtue themselves, they benefit from having some bad persons living with them. The bad provide an occasion of greater merit for the good. Their own zeal must become more fervent; they must work harder to correct the others' wrongdoing; they must endure persecution from them; they will be humbled by being lumped together with them in the opinion of others; they suffer the consequences of the wrongdoers' actions along with them. They should learn to give thanks to God, who has kept them from becoming the kind of people who do evil, lest they become such. *Whatever a man sows, that he will also reap;* if good people lack the occasions for virtue that come to them from living with the bad, to that extent their merits will be reduced.

Gal. 6:7

15. Those who behave badly are not to be favored or preferred in the community, but they should be tolerated, especially when their wrongdoing is unknown and has not affected others, and when there is still hope

for their correction. If they do not meet these conditions, however, keeping them in the community will do serious harm. They should be expelled. Otherwise it will be supposed that the good members of the community condone their misbehavior.

Even while their misconduct is being tolerated, however, wrongdoers ought to be subjected to penalties, admonished, corrected, shamed, and punished. They should also be soothed by exhortations and words of comfort. The head should pray with them and promise them better treatment if they recover from their moral frailty and become strong. Close every avenue of sin to them; keep temptation away from them— that is even beneficial for the good, who may be weakened by opportunities to do wrong.

The head of a community is God's representative, *whom the Master will set over his household;* his subordinates obey him because he has the Lord's place. He will render a heavy account to the Lord if he does not correct the delinquent, if he allows vices and evil customs to grow up under his government, or lets those that have already arisen grow stronger and spread. If he sees that the kind of life required by the rule of the community is not being lived and that transgressions are becoming more numerous, he must do what he can to overcome both the present evils and those that threaten.

Luke 12:42

16. If a head neglects these duties, he will render account to God on three points.

First, he was guilty of neglect in not doing what his duty called for. *Because as servants of his kingdom you did not rule rightly, nor keep the law, nor walk according to the purpose of God, he will come upon you terribly and swiftly, because severe judgment falls on those in highest places.*

Wis. 6:5-6

Second, he bears the guilt for all the faults of his subordinates, because he could and should have cor-

Ezek. 33:8 rected them and issued warnings about them. *If I say to the wicked, O wicked man, you shall surely die, and you do not speak to warn the wicked to turn from his way, that wicked man shall die in his iniquity, but his blood I will require at your hand.*

Third, he has abused the honor and the power that belong to his position by perverting them to his own glory and advantage, rather than employing them in *Matt.* their true purpose. *Take the talent from him . . . and* *25:28-30* *cast the worthless servant into the outer darkness; there men will weep and gnash their teeth.*

17. But a good head, zealous for righteousness, shows how much he loves God by doing the will of God himself and by fostering submission to God's will in others. His zeal does not grow tame in idleness, nor does his labor wear him out. Bad advice does not turn him from the right path, nor does trickery get around him. Neither friendship nor flattery change his purpose, nor do threats scare him. He does not lose hope, even when he must confront the same bad habits every day, but sticks to his task.

CHAPTER THREE

BROTHERLY LOVE

1. The second quality that one who is in charge of a Christian community needs is brotherly love, or compassion. Just as the love of God inflames his zeal for righteousness, affection for his brethren should form him in brotherly love. *Thy rod and thy staff they com-* *Ps. 23:5* *fort me. What do you wish? Shall I come to you with a* *1 Cor. 4:21* *rod, or with love in a spirit of gentleness?* Let the rod strike down vice; it is just as necessary for the staff to sustain weakness.

The good Samaritan, finding the victim of the bandits *Luke 10:33* lying abandoned and only half alive, poured oil and wine on his wounds. When a member of the community needs help, the head should offer the wine of fervent zeal and the oil of comforting brotherly love.

2. Both physical and mental weaknesses may affect the members of a Christian community. The weaknesses are different, but each needs our compassion.

Physical Weakness

Physical infirmities take three forms. First come those who are bedridden with chronic or acute illnesses. Then there are the housebound and others who can walk outside from time to time, but suffer from chronic disabling conditions. Lastly, some are frail and weak from age or weakness, although they have no definite illness, or they are constitutionally prone to temporary exhaustion and sickness.

A loving head will provide help for these afflicted individuals in three ways: by getting appropriate medical attention for them; by reducing the austerity of their lives with respect to fasts, vigils, garb and the like; and by exempting them to whatever extent is necessary from the tasks, services, studies and so on to which the members of the community are ordinarily obliged. According to the need of each, let the head provide remedies for the most urgent needs first.

3. One must show every kindness to the sick and enfeebled, because they are suffering at the Lord's hands. If, on top of that, they endure tribulation from men, their very misery will cry aloud to the Father of *Ps. 69:26* mercies, against those who trouble them: *they persecute him whom thou hast smitten, and him whom thou hast wounded they afflict still more.* A sick person cannot help himself in his afflicted condition, and is all the more troubled if those who are committed to him do not console him, relieve him from his work, provide for *Ps. 69:20-21* his needs, or have compassion on him. *Insults have broken my heart, so that I am in despair. I looked for pity, but there was none; and for comforters, but I found none. They gave me poison for food, and for my thirst they gave me vinegar to drink.*

4. A good head knows that he is the father, not the lord, of his brothers, and shows himself their physician, rather than their tyrant. He does not think of them as cattle or slaves, to be purchased, but as sons and fellow heirs with him of a supernatural inheritance. He should *Matt. 7:12* treat them as he wishes others to treat him were he in the same need. Strong, healthy people do not have the same feelings as the invalid; they do not know how to appreciate their sufferings. They will understand later when they have pains of their own.

Some may object that the sick often pretend to be more enfeebled than they are, and therefore suggest that they should be treated as hypocrites. The Lord, on the contrary, chose to spare many evil men for the sake of the few righteous. The good head will do his best for all the sick, those who complain too much along with the rest.

Gen. 18:23-33

5. There are three reasons why the infirm need more loving help than the healthy and robust. First, they cannot obtain by themselves the necessities of life. If they do not receive physical sustenance from others, they cannot survive. *God will not take away the life of him who devises means not to keep his banished one an outcast.*

2 Sam. 14:14

Second, in their infirmity they have lost their health and strength. Those who are healthy and strong need sustenance only in order to keep what they have. The sick and weak need help for two purposes: to avoid losing whatever strength they still have, and to recover what they have lost. *From him who has not, even what he has will be taken away.*

Luke 19:26

Finally, the help they receive is itself a relief for their troubles. For it comforts them in their many afflictions to see that others have compassion for them and can be counted on to assist them in their efforts at recovery. *May you be blessed by the Lord; for you have had compassion on me.*

1 Sam. 23:21

6. Some say that it is proper to help invalids who have some hope of recovery, but a useless expense in cases where no recovery can be expected. There would be point to that argument if the merciful love that one owes to the infirm were based on human advantages and not on the value of divine love. In fact, a person who takes care of the infirm in order to be repaid after they recover health deprives himself of the merit of charity. The more generous our mercy and the more unselfish our charity, the more clearly do we show

Luke 6:34-35

ourselves to be merciful and charitable, rather than calculating.

Heb. 4:15   *We have not a high priest who is unable to sympathize with our weaknesses.* It is even beneficial for the head to experience the same infirmities as the rest sometimes, for he learns to have compassion on them.

Spiritual Weakness

7. Spiritual infirmities also fall into three categories. Lack of spiritual commitment, or an impulsive yielding to temptation, makes some individuals prone to scandalous behavior, wrongdoing, vacillation from good *1 Cor. 11:30*   courses to evil, and a tendency to lapses. *Many of you are weak and ill.*

There are others who are devout and well-intentioned, but weak. A mild disagreement or, still more, a strong objection hinders them from doing the good they desire. Then they either become hopelessly discouraged or so angry as to cause a serious commotion. Later they are sorry, but others in the community *Rom. 15:1*   have been disturbed: *We who are strong ought to bear with the failings of the weak.*

Finally there are many imperfect persons who vacillate in their efforts to be virtuous. They feel in themselves, even if unwillingly, the fevers of the passions—anger, laziness, self-exaltation, pride, lust, *Ps. 6:2*   and other fleshly and spiritual vices. *Be gracious to me, O Lord, for I am languishing.*

8. Three remedies must be provided for these failings. First, deny such people any opportunity to give scandal or do wrong. To keep them from hearing or seeing anything that may weaken their wills, prevent them from often going out on their own away from the community.

Next, give them a good example of patience, and at the same time keep up their courage by frequent exhor-

tations. Until they recover from their infirmities, spare
them from harsh rebukes and any other treatment
which might further offend or distress them. *Do not*   Col. 3:21
provoke your children, lest they become discouraged.
Indeed, to further disturb an already disturbed person
is like provoking a barking dog into biting.

Finally, learn to put up with their minor imperfec-
tions and personal habits without becoming disturbed,
recognizing that we cannot all do everything.   Sir. 17:30

9. Learned individuals are lenient toward mistakes
made by the ignorant and unskilled; so too, people of
tried virtue kindly put up with the defects of others,
knowing that everyone cannot be equally perfect. They
do not burden those who are young and immature in
Christ with more than they can endure, nor do they
demand of them what exceeds their strength. *My lord*   Gen. 33:13
knows that the children are frail, and that the flocks
and herds giving suck are a care to me; and if they are
overdriven for one day, all the flocks will die. These
immature little ones have definite good will; but do not
drive them to conform to a stricter standard of virtue
than they have the grace for. That will extinguish what
grace they have by making them more agitated than
their spiritual strength can sustain. *We were gentle*   1 Thess. 2:7
among you, like a nurse taking care of her children;
that is to say, I am humble, kind and mild with you,
asking no more than the weak and imperfect can do.

The Lord has a quarrel with shepherds who are harsh
and lack compassion: *The weak you have not*   Ezek. 34:4
strengthened, the sick you have not healed, the crip-
pled you have not bound up, the strayed you have not
brought back, the lost you have not sought, and with
force and harshness you have ruled them. Bernard of
Clairvaux says, "Learn how to be mothers to those
under your headship, not lords; study how to be loved
rather than feared. If at times only severity can do the
job, let it be not a tyrant's but a father's severity. Prove

yourselves to be mothers by the way you foster those under your care; by the way you correct them prove that you are fathers. Be mild, not harsh; restrain yourself from blows, and offer comfort. Be filled with the milk of human kindness, not swollen with rage. Why make your yoke weigh so heavy upon them, when you should

Num. 11:12 be carrying their burdens?"[1] *Carry them in your bosom, as a nurse carries a suckling child, to the land which thou didst swear to give their fathers.*

---

[1]*On the Song of Songs*, Sermon 23, n. 2.

CHAPTER FOUR

PATIENCE

1. The third virtue a head needs is unwavering patience, or long-suffering. In order to keep the interior of the temple clean, there had to be a roof to bear dust, rain and gusts of wind. In the same way, leaders faithfully defend those under their headship from the storms of sin. To do so, they must often expose themselves to the force of various adversities, as a mother hen will battle a bird of prey to protect her children.

Exod. 26:7; 35:11

The Need for Patience

2. There are three principal reasons why the head needs a great deal of patience. First, many responsibilities, time-consuming activities, and fatiguing tasks demand his attention. For he is responsible for both the spiritual and physical welfare of the members of the community. We see that Paul was anxious to meet not only the spiritual, but also the temporal needs of the faithful, especially of the poor: *James and Cephas and John ... would have us remember the poor, which very thing I was eager to do.* The Lord himself fed those who had received the word of salvation with ordinary bread that they needed but could not obtain.

Gal. 2:9-10

Mark 6:35-44; 8:1-10

The many time-consuming activities of headship derive from both the community's internal concerns

25

and its dealings with the outside. To some extent, a head must take thought for these things even if it causes him anxiety, for he is the person responsible for them.

The fatiguing tasks of headship include business dealings, journeys, and other jobs that will often keep one busy late into the night, demanding much patience. Moses, meek and close to God as he was, wanted to give up the burden of governing Israel on this account, for he felt unable to handle the task. *How can I bear alone the weight and burden of you and your strife? Choose wise, understanding and experienced men according to your tribes, and I will appoint them as your heads.*

Deut. 1:12-13

3. A head also needs patience when he sees how little return he gets for all his labor. For even though he wears himself out, he will not see much spiritual growth in the community. He may try many things and finally, after much labor, find the people under him beginning to improve a little. But so many obstacles stand in the way of spiritual progress that they will easily be delayed again. A head may be tempted to despair of ever seeing a return for his labors; he is like a farmer who sows much but reaps a poor harvest.

Hag. 1:6

At times, a head will even see that rules he personally established are neglected and that his orders are carelessly obeyed. Often he will find evil conduct stealing into the community under the appearance of good. Something will appear to be good, so that he dares not denounce it as evil, but in reality it destroys some greater good and opens the door for more obvious evils.

For example, a sincere desire to save many souls may lead a monastic community to accept more members than it can properly manage. That very multiplication of its numbers then hinders the community's observance of poverty. More of the members will want to enjoy more good things rather than live simply. From

that follow more frequent business dealings to acquire
the necessities of life. Soon the community is trying
unusual methods for raising money and accepting gifts
that the rule prohibits. Thus, the peace of a devout life
disappears, while the community's religious standards
lie neglected. The members begin aimlessly travelling
around, hunting out various provisions for the flesh.   *Rom. 13:14*
They enter relationships prohibited by the rule; they
look for gifts from those who seek their advice; they
curry favor with the rich. They give up tasks that would
strengthen other Christians in return for opportunities
to beg. They expand their properties, build sumptuous
residences, but do not cure scandals. Such activities
crush the honor of God underfoot—that honor which a
community ought to advance by its holy conduct and
the inspiration it gives to its neighbors.

A similar abuse occurs when young men, and men
whose virtue has not been seriously tested, are prema-
turely ordained or given responsibility for community
leadership, preaching and counselling.

In short, many things can be done that look good to
human opinion, but actually stain our once pure interior devotion to God. Some people in the community,
being dull and imperceptive about the interior life,
may even suppose that all the power of a spiritual way
of life lies in the external appearance of greatness.
Accordingly, they defend such practices with great
zeal, while neglecting true virtues and genuinely
spiritual matters.

These and similar abuses will cause a spirit-filled
head profound disappointment and pain. Since he is
unable to correct all these problems even though he
longs to do so, he has great need of patience. *My zeal*   *Ps. 119:139*
consumes me. . . . Zeal for thy house has consumed   *Ps. 69:9*
me. . . .

4. A third reason why a head needs patience is the
ungratefulness of those he works and cares for. His

charges are scarcely ever satisfied with him; rather, they always feel put upon, because they are sure that he could do things differently, and better, if he wished. Often one is perplexed, not knowing whether to yield to their constant demands and allow everything they want, or to hold firmly to the course of action that one believes will do more good: *Which I shall choose I cannot tell. I am hard pressed between the two.*

Phil. 1:22-23

Many things that a head does are twisted by his people and given a bad interpretation. They murmur at his decisions, make accusations against him, reveal his faults, and derive matter for scandal from things that he did out of a sense of duty to God and to them. It is almost impossible to escape the fact that whatever one determines or does, it will upset some of the brethren. Some will go so far as to resist their head to his face or argue with him in writing. They scorn him and rouse others to oppose him, or else find clever ways to keep him from fulfilling his duties.

The Shield of Patience

5. To stand up against these conflicts, and others which will confront him, a head needs a shield of threefold patience. First, he must know how to answer everyone modestly, maturely and kindly, so that he can stop overheated attacks without showing impatience in his speech or expression—without, in fact, even developing an impatient outlook. His patience will gain him more ground, and finally win over those who would only be further provoked by impetuous action. Thus Gideon gave a modest answer when the men of Ephraim reproached him, and so pacified the bitter anger stirring within them. *A soft answer turns away wrath, but a harsh word stirs up anger.* After all, a disturbance will hardly be calmed by further disturbance, nor does one vice cure another.

Judg. 8:1-3

Prov. 15:1

A head who does become impatient upsets the good
he could have achieved. Impatience has a number of
bad results. It scandalizes others: *He who has a hasty*   *Prov. 14:29*
temper exalts folly. It renders a person contemptible to
those in his charge and to other people as well: *The one*   *Prov. 12:8*
of perverse mind is despised. It makes a person hateful
and dreaded: *A man who is reckless in speech will be*   *Sir. 9:18*
hated.

Impatience also provokes others to impatience: *The*   *Prov. 15:18*
hot-tempered man stirs up strife, but he who is slow to
anger quiets contention. It makes the members of the
community afraid to go to the head with their needs: *If*   *Job 4:2*
one ventures a word with you, will you be offended? As
a result, the community is filled with murmuring and
rancor: *He who troubles his household will inherit the*   *Prov. 11:29*
wind, "wind" meaning "conspiracies." An impatient
head scares off the simple members and makes them
timid.[1] Then no one will dare to warn him when some-
thing requires correction: *He is so ill-natured that one*   *1 Sam. 25:17*
cannot speak to him.

6. Next, a head of a community should try to be a
peacemaker—the second way in which patience is a
shield. He should not avenge injuries done to him, nor
hate those who inflict the injuries, nor hesitate to work
for their cure. He should be glad to keep ungrateful
persons in the community, for he will strengthen both
these and other members by so doing good to them. He
himself will grow in virtue through such persons, as our
supreme Shepherd says: *You will be sons of the Most*   *Luke 6:35*
High, for he is kind to the ungrateful and the selfish.

Leaders should not try to separate such people from
themselves. It is, after all, the shepherd's chief duty to
teach virtuous living. What good will it do to remove

---

[1]Bonaventure quotes Prov. 18:14, which in the Vulgate, because of
an error, reads, "Who can endure the spirit of one who is easily
angered?"

from his care the very people who most need his help? If the doctor runs away from the sick, who will heal them? If a soldier shuns the attack, how will he taste victory? If a business man neglects the deals which offer most profit, how will he get rich? This is the reason why many bishops, pastors and religious superiors become saints: the nature of their duties gives them opportunity to do much good, to suffer many adversities, and to lead others to the heights of perfec-

1 Tim 3:1 — tion. *If anyone aspires to the office of bishop, he desires a noble task.*

7. The third aspect of the shield of patience is perseverance. Whatever his difficulties, the head must be willing and eager to do everything that his duties require. Sometimes this work is exhausting, its progress is slow, the members of the community are demanding, and there are other burdens. Yet all these obstacles can

2 Chron. 15:7 — lead to high merit. *But you, take courage! Do not let your hands be weak, for your work shall be rewarded.* The "hands" of a leader are determination in getting his job done and patience in bearing burdens. If they are not weakened by laziness or impatience, their eternal reward will constantly increase.

8. The adversities that a head undergoes can actually carry several advantages. For one thing, if his human weakness has entangled him in wrongdoing, his

James 3:2 — hardships cleanse him of its effects. *For we all make many mistakes.* Where there is much to do, much is often neglected. Leaders, therefore, need to be cleansed here, so that they need not be punished

2 Sam. 7:14 — hereafter. *When he commits iniquity, I will chasten him with the rod of men, with the stripes of the sons of men.*

9. Adversity also protects one from the swelling of pride, which is more insidious for those in authority. The high position, the extent of one's freedom and the gratification of doing good work might easily make one

proud. But the yoke of adversity bows down the neck of presumption, and thus defends the head from the yawning gulf of pride. *Then he opens the ears of men, that he may turn man aside from his deed, and cut off pride from man; he keeps back his soul from the Pit, his life from perishing by the sword. Man is also chastened with pain upon his bed, and with continual strife in his bones.*

Job 33:16-19

A good head's own salvation and spiritual progress are protected by humbling adversity; without it, success would lift him up on the wind of presumption. David, a man after God's own heart, was humble and very fervent as long as he was hard pressed by trouble: *It is good for me that I was afflicted, that I might learn thy statutes.* But when prosperity raised him up, he fell into sin.

Ps. 119:71

10. A head's holiness, as we said before, increases through both the good he does and the evil he suffers. It is glorious to do good and to inspire others to do good. To suffer adversities leads to a magnificent crown, as gold that is tried in the fire becomes more beautiful and more precious.

Wis. 3:6

In fact, spiritual progress is often made when one does not feel the increase, and one is strengthened while seeming to grow more infirm. *The kingdom of God is as if a man should scatter seed upon the ground, and should sleep and rise night and day, and the seed should sprout and grow, he knows not how.*

Mark 4:26-27

It is little wonder that not all the head's efforts lead to profit for everyone; even God, who works in all men, does not succeed in bringing about the salvation of every human being. *Many are called but few are chosen.* Not every seed that is sown comes to fruition, and those who dig for treasure willingly tear up large tracts of land to find a little gold and silver. The true effect of a good head can be measured by the amount of harm that would befall the community without him. Headship is

Matt. 22:14

like light, so good to have that its mere absence is an
evil.

This truth should encourage the one over a community to bear up under his work load, for he serves God
just as faithfully in giving headship to those who make
little or no progress as in giving it to those who do the
best. *Each shall receive his wages according to his* 1 Cor. 3:8
labor, and it is *only God who gives the growth.* Just as 1 Cor. 3:7
goods that are much harder to make sell for more, so a
farmer who labors over sterile and rocky soil, gets only
a small crop, but can often ask a higher price. A teacher,
too, works harder with a pupil who will not learn than
with one who will, and so on, to a just judge, his labor is
more meritorious.

CHAPTER FIVE

GOOD EXAMPLE

1. The life of the head should be a model to the rest of the community. What his words teach his actions ought to show, as the diagrams drawn by a geometry teacher illustrate his proofs. *Jesus began to do and teach. I have given you an example, that you also should do as I have done to you. Look at me, and do likewise.*

Acts 1:1
John 13:15
Judg. 7:17

The head of a Christian community should give an example of all the virtues to the people under his authority. There are three ways especially in which he can give such an example: by conforming himself to the observance of everything that makes up the community's life, humbly showing kindness to all people, and conducting himself with mature honesty. *Show yourself in all respects a model of good deeds, and in your teaching show integrity, gravity and sound speech that cannot be censured.*

Titus 2:7-8

Observing the Common Life

2. The first of the three ways to give good example is by sharing the same standard of living as the rest of the community with respect to clothing, food, and work. The head ought not to relax with a nice drink among his guests while everyone else is restricted to plain food

and beverages. Nor should he dress differently from the rest, since he shares with them the same commitment. As the one who directs the members of a community in their daily work, he ought not to avoid taking a share in it. For if the shepherd cuts himself out of the flock, he exposes the sheep to the tricks of the wolves.

Instead, the head should be strong with the strong and weak with the weak; *To the weak I became weak,* as an example for them, *that I might win the weak. I have become all things to all men, that I might by all means save some.* For if a strong man lives as though he were frail, other strong people in the community follow his example and begin to indulge the flesh. But if a sick man refuses to take appropriate remedies, he intimidates other sick people by suggesting either that he wants them to do likewise, or that he does not desire their recovery. A soldier is more quick to the battle line if he sees his leader enduring the toil of the struggle along with him.

1 Cor. 9:22

The apostles were aware of the importance of our Lord's example to them *during all the time that the Lord Jesus went in and out among us, beginning from the baptism of John until the day when he was taken up from us.* That is, from the time that the Lord first took disciples after his baptism, right up until the moment he ascended to the Father, he always taught them by his own example. *He went in,* living with his disciples as his family, and *he went out,* giving valuable teachings to the crowds that gathered.

Acts 1:21-22

Humility

3. It is also important for the head to be humble in his conduct. Let his behavior show that he does not think too highly of himself, nor assumes the airs of an official. It should be clear that he fears his role, that he retains his responsibilities because he is required to do

so, and would prefer to be subordinate rather than to rule. He should also show that he considers those in his charge better than himself, and would rather regard himself as a servant than as a lord or master. *Let the* *greatest among you become as the youngest, and the* *leader as one who serves . . . I am among you as one* *who serves. If they make you master of the feast, do not* *exalt yourself; be among them as one of them.*

Luke *22:26-27*

Sir. 32:1

4. A humble man sees to it that members of the community have ready access to him. He is pleasant-spoken, so that they can discuss their needs with him trustfully. He listens patiently, does every kindness he can, and offers careful instruction and prompt exhortation. He should take pains to be more loved than feared, because a beloved leader is more willingly obeyed. Loving obedience is characteristically voluntary, while fearful obedience derives from compulsion. The more voluntary our obedience, the higher its merit. Since a faithful head wants his people to develop such merits, he should seek for willing obedience. After all, the purpose of spiritual authority is to direct those in one's charge toward eternal life.

5. The head ought to show humility in his use of property and goods, neither having nor seeking luxuries. Everything he owns should show his willing acceptance of poverty and so reveal his humility. This applies to his home and room, to his furniture and appliances, his books, clothing, food and table, and whatever else he has. Nothing he owns should be showy or interesting just as a curiosity, nor should he let others in his community keep such things. For like enjoys like: lofty men delight in sublimities, but lowly men delight in lowly things. It is no sign of a humble heart to seek out curiosities, or to be ambitious to own and show off what is precious and luxurious. *He be-* *holds everything that is high; he is king over all the* *sons of pride.*

Job 41:34

Maturity

6. There are three ways a head can show his maturity. First, he should never act lightly. Thus, he avoids jokes and phrases that seem funny but are really hurtful or silly. People neither admire nor respect those who habitually indulge in such false humor. As Pope Gregory the Great observed, "It is hard to accept the preaching of someone who behaves like a trifler."[1] While a head should usually be more loved than feared, it is good for the insolent person to feel some fear toward him. Love itself is felt more strongly when combined with reverence, as is evident in our love for our Creator: the more we acknowledge his absolute majesty, the better do we love his sweet condescension. *Good and upright is the Lord; therefore he instructs sinners in the way.*

Ps. 25:8

7. Also, the head ought not to be light with his affections. He must discipline himself to avoid wrong sexual attachments or any kind of significant involvement with anyone whose character is questionable. The more faithful members of the community are to be preferred in one's affections, and everyone should be embraced in one's hope for their salvation in Christ.

A head's conduct should be such that all the members of the community trust him and confide in him as their best friend, each one taking his love for granted. He should do nothing to cause another person to feel that his head scorns him and arbitrarily prefers others. Joseph's brothers hated him just because their father had such a special love for him; never show such favoritism as to nourish indignation or envy in others.

Gen. 37

8. Finally, a head should not lightly change his plans for action or his advice. Suppose that something

---

[1]*Homilies on Ezekiel*, I, sermon 3, n. 4.

pleases him at one moment and displeases him the next, or that he wants one thing now, and later the contrary. After seeing such lack of stability, who will accept his judgment or adapt to his will? Under such circumstances, his subordinates cannot respect his prudence, nor commit themselves to obey his direction. The resulting damage may be serious. *Do all things without grumbling or questioning,* that is without hesitating and reconsidering. *Test everything; hold fast what is good.*   *Phil. 2:14*

1 Thess. 5:21

One may, of course, have good reason to alter some decisions out of real necessity or some solid religious advantage. Such changes are not a sign of levity but of maturity. It would be stupid to give up the better for the sake of the worse; it would likewise be sheer obstinacy to stick to one's first plans so stubbornly that even a great and obvious benefit could not bring one to change them. *We will take care to render our kingdom quiet and peaceable for all men, by changing our methods and always judging what comes before our eyes with more equitable consideration.*   *Est. 16:8-9*

When Paul excused himself from his promise to visit the Corinthians, he assured them that he had not changed his mind lightly, but for their own sake: *I wanted to come to you first, so that you might have a double pleasure. . . . Was I vacillating when I wanted to do this? Do I make my plans like a worldly man, ready to say yes and no at once? As surely as God is faithful, our word to you has not been yes and no. . . . But I call God to witness against me—it was to spare you that I refrained from coming to Corinth.*   *2 Cor. 1:15-23*

The head, both when upholding his previous decisions and when changing them for good reason, must bear this in mind: *like the magistrate of the people, so are his officials; and like the ruler of the city, so are all its inhabitants.*   *Sir. 10:2*

The Value of Example

9. Good masters generally form good disciples. People who see a better way of living exemplified by their instructors often become better Christians and better participants in the community's life. The head who neglects his duty to give a good example will be strictly

Ezek. 34:10   judged: *Thus says the Lord God: Behold, I am against the shepherds. I will require my sheep at their hand, and put a stop to their feeding the sheep; no longer shall the shepherds feed themselves. I will rescue my sheep from their mouths, that they may not be food for them.*

Verbal instruction unaccompanied by active good example is like mortar without lime—dry and strength-

Ezek. 13:14   less. *And I will break down the wall that you have daubed with whitewash, and bring it down to the ground, so that its foundation will be laid bare; when it falls, you shall perish in the midst of it; and you shall know that I am the Lord.* A new edition of a book can only be as correct as the older copy on which it is based. Actions speak louder than words; the lessons we teach are more firmly embedded in our deeds than in our speech. "A man's preaching is despised if his way of life is worthy of scorn."[2]

The head ought to commit himself with special determination to forming those in his charge according to the pattern of Christ. This means that he imprints on them the way of life and the doctrine of Christ. He seeks to lead them to imitate the Lord in every aspect of

Eph. 5:1   their lives, not just to refer to him in their thoughts. *Be*
Gal. 4:19   *imitators of God, as beloved children. My little children, with whom I am again in travail until Christ be formed in you.* But verbal instruction by itself is not enough to convey the whole teaching of Christ.

---

[2]Gregory the Great, *Homilies on Ezekiel*, I, sermon 12, n. 1.

Leaders, therefore, should be visible models of Christ's way of life, so that they can imprint it more deeply on their people. *Be imitators of me, as I am of* *1 Cor. 11:1* *Christ.* That is to say, if you want to be molded into the form of Christ, look carefully at my way of life: *It is no* *Gal. 2:20* *longer I who live, but Christ who lives in me.* For the head of the community does indeed rule in the place of Christ; he ought to promote whatever is pleasing to Christ, exercise Christ's authority, and be himself a model of likeness to Christ.

In this way, a head should encourage those in his charge to do the Lord's will. With the Lord's authority, he should serve his people in everything that will benefit them, and make his own life an example that they may safely imitate. *For what we preach is not our-* *2 Cor. 4:5* *selves, but Jesus Christ as Lord, with ourselves as* *your servants for Jesus' sake.* When a head's speech promotes his own glory, he preaches himself, not Christ. When he gives an example of bad conduct, he encourages his charges to imitate him rather than Christ. *They* *Gal. 4:17* *make much of you, but for no good purpose; they want* *to shut you out, that you may make much of them.* This means that heads whose evil examples shut you out from the imitation of Christ act from no good motive. They want you to learn to follow their own wrong way of life.

CHAPTER SIX

GOOD JUDGMENT

1. Discernment—the ability to make prudent judgments on all actions—is the fifth virtue needed for spiritual leadership. Solomon shows how urgent is the need of it. When God offered to give him whatever he asked for, he ignored every other possibility to ask for wisdom. Without it, he declared, no king could rule his people well. *Give thy servant therefore an understanding mind to govern thy people, that I may discern between good and evil; for who is able to govern this thy great people? To you then, O monarchs, my words are directed, that you may learn wisdom and not transgress. Now therefore, O kings, be wise; be warned, O rulers of the earth.*

1 Kings 3:9

Wis. 6:9

Ps. 2:10

A head is the leader of the flock committed to his charge. If he goes off the right path, his flock will scatter in confusion. As the eye is the light of the whole body, so is the shepherd to the flock committed to him: *You are the light of the world.* Depending on whether the eye sees clearly or badly, the body will be guided in a straight or weaving path.

Matt. 5:14

2. A head needs good judgment, or discernment, in order to know what to do and how to do it. For even if an activity is good in itself it will only do good when it fits the circumstances. Bernard of Clairvaux says, "Remove good judgment and virtue will become vice."[1]

41

And indeed, without discretion, zeal turns into immature and headstrong rashness: *They have a zeal for
God, but it is not enlightened.* Compassion, under the
appearance of brotherly love, declines into sentimen-
tality: *He who spares the rod hates his son, but he who
loves him is diligent to discipline him.* This means that
any leader who fails to correct sinful behavior because
he wants to show compassion is actually sending a soul
to destruction.

Rom. 10:2

Prov. 13:24

Without good judgment, patience robs authority of its
proper vigor, so that a leader supposedly acting out of
humility fails to stop rebellion: *Rehoboam was young
and irresolute and could not withstand them,* "them"
being the men who opposed his rule and God's. Even
good example loses its power to build up other Christians unless it is given with discretion, just as good food
needs salt for better taste. So do what good you can, but
show good judgment in how, when, where and why you
do it.

2 Chron. 13:7

3. So many problems demand good judgment in a
head that one cannot treat them all in a brief discussion.
There are, however, four areas that especially require
care. Provide well for these, and difficulties arising
from indiscretion will be few.

The first is governing those committed to one's
charge in a way that will help them continue to do good
and advance in holiness. Second is correcting lapsed
and misbehaving members so that they return to better
courses. Third, taking care of business and administrative matters, and all the outside affairs in which headship involves one. And fourth, governing oneself and
providing for one's own spiritual needs in the midst of
other responsibilities.

When a head accepts responsibility to care for the
souls of others, he becomes like the high priest of the

---

[1]*Sermons on the Song of Songs, 49, n. 5*

Old Testament, ministering to the Lord in the sanctuary. The high priest wore a "breastplate of judg-   *Exod. 28:15*
ment" embellished with four rows of jewels. The
four ways in in which leaders must show their good
judgment are like these rows of jewels. Their fourfold
discretion equips them to serve God in a task greatly
pleasing to him, one that furthers the salvation of souls.
For no sacrifice is more pleasing to God than zeal for
souls.

Helping People Continue in Christian Life

4. A head who sets out to help people go on living a
good Christian life needs a thorough acquaintance with
their habits, abilities, and consciences[2] so that he can
assign each person to an appropriate place in the life of
the community. For all things are not equally possible
for everyone, *but each has his own special gift from*   *1 Cor. 7:7*
God, one of one kind and one of another.

Leaders of communities, and individuals with other
pastoral duties in them, are like the high priest Aaron
and his sons: *Aaron and his sons shall go in and ap-*   *Num. 4:19*
point them each to his task and to his burden. They
ought to know the interior state of all those for whom
they are responsible, so that they can assign duties and
situations appropriate to each. This work can be divided according to three levels of importance.

5. The high priest's breastplate had four rows of
jewels, with three jewels in each row. Just as the four
rows can be taken as symbolic of the four duties of
leadership that call for good judgment, so also the three
precious stones in each row can represent three different levels of vigilance needed in fulfilling these duties.

---

[2]In speaking here of knowing the consciences of the brothers,
Bonaventure means that the head of a Christian community should
know what sort of life each has lived, and should acquaint himself
with their standards of morality and their conduct.

The first degree of vigilance is called for when one is dealing with basic commitments made by members of the community, especially those serious enough to require faithfulness at any cost. The head of a Christian community has no authority to dispense the members from commitments that they have made to the Lord so solemnly that their very salvation now depends on keeping them. And the head is just as strictly obliged to keep such vows as any other member.

An example of a very serious vow would be any commitment which, if deliberately broken, would separate either the community or the individual member from Christ. Another would be anything that so changes the life of the body that the members no longer give the Lord the kind of service which they had promised. It is deadly sin to break such vows. Thus, members of religious orders who have made permanent vows of obedience, poverty and chastity may not be dispensed from them.[3]

The head of a Christian community must be always watchful of such commitments. All the members ought to fulfill them with zeal, but the commitments must be kept even if people are reluctant to do so. The head must enforce the observance of serious vows as fully as possible, and may not allow them to be broken for any reason, even if this insistence brings great tribulation *Rom. 8:35* and loss upon the whole community. *Who shall separate us from the love of Christ? Shall tribulation, or distress, or persecution, or famine, or nakedness, or peril, or sword?* Paul intends us to answer: "None of these."

---

[3]Bonaventure here speaks of the vows of religious orders as irrevocable. This view, customary in his day, is no longer held by the Catholic Church. Also, when Bonaventure speaks of the community's commitment to give the Lord a particular type of service, he is not necessarily speaking of the kind of jobs at which community members work, but of commitments to a way of life that enables the community to offer its service.

This is the answer for those who say, "How can we sustain ourselves, how can our brethren obtain the necessities of life, when we must follow so strict a rule?" For some ways of making a living are so contradictory to the life that we promised to live for God, and bring so much disrepute upon the community, that it is better for people to leave the community than support themselves within it by those means. If those who cannot or will not live according to the community principles depart, they do not destroy their own souls, but they do cease to scandalize others. We read in Scripture: *Whoever causes one of these little ones who believe in me to sin, it would be better for him to have a great millstone fastened round his neck and to be drowned in the depth of the sea.* If the Lord considers it so evil to lead one person into sin, what is to be thought of those who tempt many?

Matt. 18:6

Considerations regarding the community's solemn commitments are always to be borne in mind more carefully than any others. The head, like the high priest with the most precious of his jewels, must protect these commitments above all.

6. The second aspect of the task of maintaining Christians in a good state is encouragement to go on to perfection. A head should encourage those committed to his charge to strive for the highest levels of patience, humility, love, and the other virtues; to be strict and simple in all their use of material goods; and to be fair and moderate in their response even to very trying circumstances. He should exhort, warn and advise his people; his good example should attract and attach them to these virtues. This is better than trying to force them to live up to some very high standard of conduct. The counsels of perfection[4] are recommendations; one persuades but does not order people to follow them.

[4]By "counsels of perfection" Bonaventure, along with other Christian writers of his time, meant specific commitments to the closest and

Only when someone has bound himself by a vow (for example, a vow of sexual continence) does the observance of one of the counsels become obligatory.

The monastic life and other forms of Christian community have been established primarily as training schools in the exercises of perfection. Training and exercise for athletic contests involves strict self-denial, a fact which Paul employs as an image of the Christian struggle: *Every athlete exercises self-control in all things.* In Paul's day, athletes who wrestled in the gymnasium stripped their bodies entirely and covered themselves with oil so that their opponents could get no grasp to throw them for a fall. That is a good image for the Christian who seeks perfection: give up everything by which the enemy of souls can get a hold on you. Add to your belongings only what will make you more successful in the struggle.

The head, therefore, should also carry this hope in his heart, like a jewel on the high priest's breast: to teach and inspire the Lord's people not only to hold to the way of salvation, but also to direct themselves to a more perfect life. This will lead him and them to the glory of heaven.

7. A third level of vigilance in exercising good judgment is needed in determining how strictly the rules of the community should be kept. These rules help one to live and grow in God's grace, but are not in themselves essential to salvation or perfection. The founders of our communities established rules to train us in good deeds, to make our communities good and happy places to live in, and to build up those who become familiar with our lives. These are the reasons for requiring fasts, times of silence, solemn forms of public worship, and other external practices which manifest our

1 Cor. 9:25 (margin)

---

most faithful discipleship, through vows of poverty, celibacy, and obedience. To "follow the life of the counsels" normally required that one join a religious order.

interior commitment. *While bodily training is of some*   1 *Tim.* 4:8
value, godliness is of value in every way. The exercises
that Paul recommends here are useful in the way that
tools are for an artisan. Experts can do more with tools
than beginners; but if need be they can even do much
without them, since their craftsmanship does not depend on the use of any particular tool.

When the need arises or a greater good can be served,
a head may at his own discretion dispense those under
him from obligations imposed by the rule of the community. This applies to regulations about times and
places for work, prayer, and various community activities. There should be no difficulty in dispensing
with such matters when a really good reason exists. On
the other hand, when neither the greater good nor real
necessity demands that allowances be made, the head
should be firm in seeing that the rules are kept.

In decisions of this nature a head needs plenty of
good judgment to know how to hold to a middle line
between strictness and laxity. Excessively strict rule
weakens the love that members of the community have
for their leader, so that when he asks them to comply
with rules in areas where compliance is indeed much
needed, or very useful, they do not do so with a good
will. If, however, he is too lenient, even greater troubles will follow, and discipline in the community will
fail completely. *He who despises small things will fail*   *Sir.* 19:1
little by little.

Correcting Misbehavior

8. A second range of responsibilities that require
the head's good judgment relates to the correction of
misbehavior. There are three different types of offender, and a leader's discretion is tested in determining
how to bring each type back into conformity with the
life of the community.

Some are ready to repent as soon as they have done anything seriously wrong. They find the remedy of penance, either through external human correction or through an internal change prompted by the Holy Spirit. With this group, the spiritual physician ought to employ the medicine of mercy. The offender should indeed act to remove whatever scandal he has given others and to repent to God for his sin. His penance ought to be severe enough to deter others from doing as he has done, but easy enough to bear that he will not regret having submitted to it. *If a man is overtaken in any trespass, you who are spiritual should restore him in a spirit of gentleness. Look to yourself, lest you too be tempted.* Those who are called "spiritual" here are like physicians who must carefully choose a suitable medicine. The penalty imposed should be stern enough to help the offender realize the seriousness of his misbehavior. But you who are responsible for imposing this penalty should act in such a merciful way that, if you were guilty of the same fault, you would be willing to undergo the same punishment.[5]

Gal. 6:1

9. Some persons, when they are guilty of any fault, conceal it, defend it, or minimize it. The sinful infection remains in them, however, even if its visible effects are few. This presents a serious problem to their head. He may recognize the signs that venom and rottenness have gathered in that part of the body even if there has been no outward eruption. He needs an opportunity to employ public correction to lance the infection, yet has no public evidence to go on so long as the guilty ones are unwilling to confess. If he rebukes the guilty, it does no good: he will have condemned

---

[5]Bonaventure is concerned here with faults that are known—and not just suspected—to the head and to other members of the community. In the next section, Bonaventure makes it clear that a head may not give public exposure to a brother's secret faults nor assign a penalty where wrongdoing is only suspected and not proved.

49

sins but not corrected sinners. If he condones what he knows is going on, he burns with anxiety for his brother's soul, and, since he did nothing about the delinquency, for his own as well.

When no better course of action offers itself, a head is well advised to wait, exercising patience and ignoring the sins that he cannot yet correct. Meanwhile, he should devote himself to prayer, a labor that may earn the conversion which his arguments cannot bring about. Perhaps at last, God will correct the individual quickly or uncover his concealed malice so that some remedy can finally be provided for it.

In the same way, our Lord silently tolerated the thief Judas for a long time, and did not openly blame him until his wickedness had increased so far that it broke out of itself into view. Even though Judas was morally sick unto death, as long as his sin remained hidden it did no harm to the souls of the rest, and so it was not blameworthy to tolerate it in silence. *Let both* [the weeds and the wheat] *grow together until the harvest.* *Let the evildoer still do evil, and the filthy still be filthy.*

The head should, however, warn the whole community whenever he can to beware of occasions of sin, so as to awaken them to their danger. We read in Scripture, *Woe to that man by whom the Son of Man is betrayed.* Yet Judas could not have committed such a terrible offense so suddenly if he had not been lapsing, little by little, into an ever worse spiritual state. So it is plain that the Lord had long been quietly putting up with his evil condition: *Have I not held my peace, even for a long time?* For a head to live and act justly, confronted by the difficulties that are brought on by the hidden sins of his brethren, demands great good judgment.

10. A third group of community members commit serious publicly known faults and refuse to accept ap-

Matt. 13:30

Rev. 22:10

Matt. 26:24

Isa. 57:11

propriate correction. Sometimes they pretend to accept the correction but do not actually improve their conduct. This is harmful to other members of the community; either they are scandalized or, seeing that the guilty are not penalized for their offenses, begin to imitate them. They expect to be spared, as they have seen others spared, even a mild correction of their wrongdoing.

A head must, therefore, consider the expulsion of an offending member if four conditions come together: the wrongdoing is serious; the offense is public; the individual's long and habitual obstinacy in wrongdoing gives one no good reason to hope that he will ever accept correction; others are being infected by his example, or scandalized by tolerance of such conduct.

If all four conditions exist, what remains but to cast the dead sheep out of the flock, to cut off the gangrenous limb? Otherwise, those who are still healthy may also be infected and corrupted. *Drive out the wicked person from among you.* When someone wants to abandon his commitments and depart from the community, let him go; indeed it is best that those who would create disturbances cut themselves off from the body. In the parable of the fig tree, our Lord represents the patience of God, who waits from year to year for the tree to bear fruit. But the time comes at last to cut down the unfruitful tree so that it may no longer burden the ground. *Even now the axe is laid to the root of the trees; every tree therefore that does not bear good fruit is cut down and thrown into the fire.*

There should, of course, be no use of physical force in such an expulsion. Let mature and prudent persons who have the gift of good counsel from the Spirit of God advise the offending member and get him to agree to leave. *Do nothing without deliberation, and when you have acted, do not regret it.*

To understand how much harm can come from the scandal given when a member of a Christian commu-

1 Cor. 5:13

Luke 13:6-9

Matt. 3:10

Sir. 32:19

nity lives an obviously sinful life, doing little good for
anyone, consider the words of our Lord: *Whoever*   *Matt. 18:6*
causes one of these little ones who believe in me to sin,
it would be better for him to have a great millstone
fastened round his neck and to be drowned in the
depth of the sea. Let the offender be put out, where he
can do the worst harm chiefly to himself, rather than
allow him to contaminate the community.

Caring for Administrative Duties

11. Administration, along with works of service,
constitutes the third type of work for which a head is
responsible. In this regard he should commit some
tasks to others and reserve some to himself. As much as
possible, however, he should avoid and excuse himself
from any superfluous duties. Thus Christ put his disciples, including Judas, in charge of obtaining the material necessities of life, while he personally retained the
duty of preaching and healing. But when he was asked
to divide an inheritance among several heirs, he an-   *Luke*
swered, *Man, who made me a judge or divider over*   *12:13-14*
you?

12. A good head delegates purely administrative responsibilities to others as much as possible. The ordinary necessities of life must indeed be taken care of,
but a head who takes charge of them himself risks
losing sight of the more important, nobler part of his
job. In his mind's eye he will tend to see less of the
interior realities that are more necessary for salvation.

We see this in Scripture: *Choose able men from all*   *Exod.*
the people, such as fear God, men who are trustworthy   *18:19-22*
and who hate a bribe. . . . And let them judge the people
at all times; every great matter they shall bring to you,
but any small matter they shall decide themselves; so it
will be easier for you, and they will bear the burden
with you. It is not right that we should give up preach-   *Acts 6:2-4*

*ing the word of God to serve tables. Therefore, breth-
ren, pick out from among you seven men of good
repute, full of the Spirit and of wisdom, whom we may
appoint to this duty. But we will devote ourselves to
prayer and to the ministry of the word.*

There are some leaders who find it easier to delegate
pastoral responsibilities than administrative work; this
is a very serious error. If the head has no one to whom
he can safely commit his temporal duties, it is better
that he even risk being defrauded in these matters
rather than devote his own attention to them. Christ has
given an example of this; knowing that Judas was a
thief, he still allowed him to make the purchases for the
John 12:6 whole group of disciples. *He was a thief, and as he had
the money box he used to take what was put into it.* It is
an incomparably greater loss to endanger souls than to
lose material possessions.

13. The head should take personal responsibility for
the spiritual concerns of his community. As their pastor
and the guardian of their souls he ought to devote his
energy chiefly to the things that pertain to spiritual
progress and eternal salvation. These matters are at the
heart of the shepherd's office.

These especially are the concerns for which a head
will render account before God's judgment seat:

The head preserves discipline within the community, so that the kind of life to which all are committed is
maintained.

He sees to it that the community lives together in
peace and love.

He should know the moral condition of every individual in the community and help each person resolve
any difficulties. He should foresee and take action
against the dangers into which his brethren may be led
by their sins. He warns the members to improve their
conduct; he throws light on doubts and corrects what
must be corrected. He gives each member suitable

formation for his work, so that everyone can do what he should for the whole community, and do it correctly, without involving himself in any wrongdoing. But when men cannot be satisfied except by offending God, we owe God our obedience; we owe only patience to men who misunderstand or find fault. *We must obey God rather than men.*   Acts 5:29

If we regard the brotherhood as a body, the one in charge is like the head. While the other members perform the actions appropriate to them, the head, being in charge of the whole, makes suitable provision for all. The head guides all the members, since all the senses—sight, hearing, touch, and so on—provide it with the necessary knowledge. The directions a leader gives, enforcing and relaxing the rules of the community, are like the coordinating functions of the body's nervous system.

The bodily head is not confined to any single specific activity, so that it can take care of the needs of all the members. It is better for every part of the body that the head hears, smells, tastes and speaks for them all. The leader of a community serves the members in a similar way: *Obey your leaders and submit to them; for they*   Heb. 13:17 *are keeping watch over your souls, as men who will have to give account. Let them do this joyfully, and not sadly, for that would be of no advantage to you.*

14. The best way to handle superfluous property, and business affairs that have no direct connection to the salvation or spiritual progress of souls, is to eliminate them. So far as possible, neither the head nor the brethren should have anything to do with such matters. The time we have to serve the Lord is short; *let the*   Matt. 6:34 *day's own trouble be sufficient for the day.* We have scarcely enough resources to take care of all that is needful. If we spend ourselves on pointless tasks or on things alien to our kind of life, we thereby neglect the more useful and better things. When we distract our-

selves, applying our energies to many different projects, we become less able to concentrate on the specific duties that are most essential.[6]

For this reason, both the head and the members of a community should avoid preoccupations and excessive involvements with buildings, studies, legal actions, and other matters; these things are foreign to our call and we live more fruitfully without them.[7] When we are taken up with them, not only do we neglect better things, but very often we fall into wrongdoing. The use of exterior things reduces the mind's ability to perceive spiritual and interior realities, so that our desire for supernatural life grows lukewarm. When the body suffers a wound, infections that set in at the site of the injury must be treated at once to prevent the development of ulcers or tumors; so too, one who lets himself become wholly taken up by distracting business affairs, which are like untreated and infected wounds, promotes his own spiritual extinction.

The wise head, therefore, ought to foresee the probable consequences of every project and set careful limits both on the business affairs that he lets the community take up and on the degree of involvement in such affairs that he permits. No more should be allowed than is clearly beneficial to the life of the community.

Sir. 11:10   *My son, do not busy yourself with many matters; if you multiply activities you will not go unpunished, and if*

[6]St. Gregory the Great gives the same teaching: "When the spirit is divided among many things, it is less able to deal with each one" (*Dialogues* I, ch. 4, see also *Pastoral Rule* I, 4).

[7]Bonaventure here condemns commitment of time and energy to matters that can only distract individuals or the community from the primary religious commitments to personal conversion, worship, common life, apostolate, and Christian service. This does not forbid all involvement in social projects, secular careers, or cultural pursuits. Bonaventure is concerned only to condemn any elements of individual or community life-style that would dissipate energies and multiply projects unnecessarily.

you pursue you will not overtake, and by fleeing you will not escape. He is a careless steward in the Lord's house who, when he already bears a heavy load in his proper work, takes on several extra burdens that he could well do without.

Governing Oneself

15. Most important of all, a head ought to guard his own spiritual life, lest while he provides for others he should neglect himself, or while helping others to find salvation he should submerge himself in danger. *For what will it profit a man, if he gains the whole world and forfeits his life? Look to yourselves, that you may not lose what you have worked for, but may win a full reward.* This is the fourth order of the head's responsibilities, and it calls for self-examination in three areas.

Matt. 16:26

2 John 8

16. The first aspect of good judgment concerning oneself regards the peace of one's own conscience. A head ought to be able to say, in examining his conscience, that his actions are honorable and his motives pure. For the security of his conscience, he should not desire, do, order, or allow anything contrary to his commitments in the community, anything that violates decency and law, nor anything involving sin or scandal. If his conscience is to be clean, he must be sure that he never does or encourages good deeds for the sake of any human glory or self-gratification, but only to please God. Whatever a head does for God, as one who acts in his name, he should also do for God's sake, out of love for him. *If your eye is sound, your whole body will be full of light.* That is, if love purifies the intention with which you act—which is the "eye" or focus of the activity—then the whole "body" of the action will earn the reward of eternal light. *But if your eye is not sound, your whole body will be full of darkness.*

Matt. 6:22

Matt. 6:23

The head should therefore study his conscience ex-
actingly; with care he should determine what he has
done, where he has failed, and what his real goals were
in doing good. When he has examined his conscience
he ought to repent of any evils he has discovered, confess them and correct them. If he sees that he has done

1 Cor. 1:31   good, he should take care to glorify the Lord for it and
not himself. Like Christ, his master, a head vigilantly
cleanses the feet of others; but he cannot enter the

Luke 4:23   Lord's house unless he cleanses his own. *Physician,
heal yourself.*

When a head thinks of the good he has done, he can
rejoice without growing proud if he bears this consideration in mind: it was not for his own sake, but on
behalf of those for whom he is responsible, that God has
granted him the power to understand correctly, to
speak well, or to do good.

17. The second aspect of a head's life that demands
good judgment is his conduct and speech when he is
engaged in serving others rather than himself. As one
whose life is devoted to other people, he must always
give a good example, meeting the needs of each person
while pleasing all. His task is complex and requires that
he maintain a golden mean, eating neither too much nor
too little, being neither immoderately gloomy nor jolly,
weighty nor superficial, solitary nor social, silent nor a
chatterer. He should speak without flattery or excessive harshness, and ought to be neither unreasonably
strict nor slack in enforcing the rule. He should not
avoid meeting with the community's guests, nor spend
too much time with them. He should neither keep a
suspicious watch on the activities of the brothers nor
disregard them; should show neither favoritism nor
prejudice.

It is, of course, impossible always to maintain the
perfect balance, and so the course that consistently
achieves the best results is to be as kind as possible.

Kindness leads the members of the community to love
their head better, obey him more willingly, turn to him
more promptly with their problems, and follow his lead
more quickly. His authority in the community is
enough to make them fear him. If he is harsh and austere
in addition, timid brothers will find his headship a
heavy burden. *The weak you have not strengthened,*   *Ezek. 34:4-5*
the sick you have not healed, the crippled you have not
bound up, the strayed you have not brought back, the
lost you have not sought, and with force and harshness
you have ruled them. So they were scattered, because
there was no shepherd; and they became food for all
the wild beasts. Do not be like a lion in your home, nor   *Sir. 4:30*
be a faultfinder with your servants.

For this reason, the chief of all shepherds, Our Lord
Jesus, showed his love to us with much kindness, so
that we would love and follow him. Our love for him as
a man then drew us to know and love his divinity, "so
that, while we come to know God in visible form, we
are drawn by him to the love of his invisible nature."[8]

For the same reason, the head of a community, as
Christ's representative, ought to do his best to earn the
willing love of those in his charge, so that he can more
readily draw them to the love of Christ. In every doubt-
ful case he should incline more to whatever choices
will truly do the most for humility and charity, and to
whatever decisions fit in best with pure gospel virtue.

18. Finally, a head must use discretion in trusting
his own good judgment. Unlike the bodily eye, which
sees everything except itself, the wisdom which makes
all judgments about everything for a community's life
must not fail to judge itself as well. Otherwise, the head
will *think of himself more highly than he ought* and   *Rom. 12:3*
become one of *those who are wise in their own eyes,*   *Isa. 5:21,*
and shrewd in their own sight! Gregory the Great has   *see also*
     Rom. 11:25

---

[8]Preface for the Christmas season, Roman Missal.

observed, "the temptation of members of the community is to condemn the leader for every single mistake he may make. Likewise leaders are tempted to consider *Prov. 26:12* themselves wiser than the rest."[9] *Do you see a man who is wise in his own eyes? There is more hope for a fool than for him.* For a foolish man, not trusting himself, will avoid deception by seeking wise men's advice. But a person who has too much confidence in his own ability often thinks he is right even when he is wrong!

Of all temptations, that which seems most dangerous for any Christian is to think too highly of his own opinion. For no one can be found, no matter how perceptive, who never falls into error. Those who regard their own view as wholly and exclusively right leave themselves open to any enemy clever enough to make a bad project seem attractive. The devil is most eager to worm his way in where he recognizes that people are trying to live virtuously; he wants to seek out the innocent man and destroy him just where he was hoping to give *Ps. 10:8* himself to God's service. *He sits in ambush in the villages; in hiding places he murders the innocent.* The head, therefore, should take care to listen willingly to advice, and to seek it humbly.

19. There is a threefold value to seeking advice.

First, when others agree with the head's decision, he can be more confident that he has made no mistake. Then again, if something should go wrong, even though he followed the advice he received, he will not be wholly to blame as he would be had he acted completely on his own. Finally, when a head humbly seeks advice, God often grants him an understanding that he lacked before. This may come from another's counsel or from his own thinking.

Exod. 33:11 Thus Moses, who spoke face to face with God, sought *Exod. 18:18* advice from Jethro, his father-in-law, and found it help-

---

[9]*Moral Reflections on Job* XXXIV, c. 23, n. 50

ful. Thus too the apostle Paul, a man who was filled
with the Holy Spirit and who had received the Gospel
message from a revelation by Jesus Christ, was prompt-
ed by the same Jesus to go to Jerusalem and discuss his   *Gal. 2:1-10*
preaching with Peter, James, and John so that he could
make sure that his message did not differ from theirs. In
doing so he gave an example to faithful leaders, that
they too should seek advice. *A man of judgment will*   *Sir. 32:18-19*
not overlook an idea. . . . Do nothing without delibera-
tion; and when you have acted, do not regret it.

Some men, however, when promoted to a governing
position, imagine that they are continually filled with
the spirit of knowledge, and that all the actions of their
predecessors were stupid and perverse. Others, once
they leave such a position, begin to condemn whatever
their successors do. They pay no attention to the fact
that, as they despised the actions of others, so the new
heads may despise theirs. *Woe to you! . . . when you*   *Isa. 33:1*
have ceased to destroy, you will be destroyed. The
person who judged the actions of others severely will
find that others watch what he does very carefully indeed; they look for the faults in his conduct that he
always found in others.

20. A prudent head should be reluctant to take advice from either flatterers or slanderers. Flatterers will
fool him into thinking more of himself than is good.
They assure him that he is blessed in order to keep him
from the truth about himself, when humility would   *Isa. 3:12*
have given him real self-knowledge. Slanderers lead a
person to suspect others of worse conduct than is true;
often they bring about the condemnation of innocent
people, or at least a wrong decision, before the truth is
fully known. *Often many of those who are set in places*   *Est. 16:5-6*
of authority have been made in part responsible for the
shedding of innocent blood, and have been involved in
irremediable calamities, by the persuasion of friends
who have been entrusted with the administration of

public affairs, when these men by the false trickery of their evil natures beguile the sincere good will of their sovereigns.

There are three common situations in which one ought to seek advice. When there is a question of improving the life of the community, one should consult with those most prudent in judgment, in order to settle any doubts about the right course of action. When it is necessary to back up a decision by showing that a strong authority supports it, one should consult men of deserved prominence. If a consultation is held to ensure the community's peace and prevent any members from having occasion for murmuring at a decision, then all who are directly concerned in the decision should be consulted.

There are, however, innumerable special situations where good judgment is necessary. One cannot, therefore, give absolute rules about when and from whom to seek advice.

CHAPTER SEVEN

DEVOTION TO GOD

1. Devotion to God is the sixth virtue of Christian headship—the last, yet the most necessary, for all the other virtues depend on it. Love for God gives us zeal for good deeds, strengthens our patience, and clarifies our judgment. It is the foundation of all good example and the motive for brotherly compassion. Love of God is a spiritual anointing that teaches us everything that leads to salvation. *The anointing which you received* 1 John 2:27 from the Holy Spirit *abides in you, and you have no need that anyone should teach you; as his anointing teaches you about everything.*

2. Thus we see that devotion to God sheds light on our decisions: *The Counselor, the Holy Spirit, whom* John 14:26 *the Father will send in my name, he will teach you all things, and bring to your remembrance all that I have said to you.* It fires us with longing for the good: *Those* Sir. 24:21 *who eat me will hunger for more, and those who drink me will thirst for more.* It gives us strength to go on to perfection: *for God is at work in you both to will and to* Phil. 2:13 *work for his good pleasure.* It makes us disgusted with sin: *I hate and abhor falsehood, but I love thy law.* It Ps. 119:163 makes us act virtuously.

Devotion to God makes us act according to our words: *Be consistent in your thoughts; stead-* Sir. 5:12 *fast be your words.* It gives a sweet savor to the

61

Sir. 6:23 knowledge that comes from faith: *For the wisdom of doctrine is according to her name.*[1] It gives us hope and
Rom. 8:16 confidence in God: *It is the Spirit himself bearing witness with our spirit that we are children of God.* And devotion to God itself grows within us, so that we
Rom. 5:5 love God the more: *God's love has been poured into our hearts through the Holy Spirit which has been given to us.*

Devotion enables us to have a close personal rela-
Exod. 33:11 tionship with God: *The Lord used to speak to Moses face to face, as a man speaks to his friend.* Our prayers
1 John 3:21-22 of petition grow more confident: *We have confidence before God, and we receive from him whatever we ask.* And those prayers attain a new anointing and
Ps. 20:3 strength: *May he remember all your offerings, and regard with favor your burnt sacrifices.*

Those who are filled with love of God become more loving themselves, for the spirit of wisdom is
Wis. 7:23 *beneficent, humane, steadfast.* Their hearts grow
Isa. 66:2 humble: *I will look* to the man *that is humble and contrite in spirit.* Their spirits are as lively as oil bubbling in a pan. They stand firm in the face of adversity:
Ps. 27:1 *The Lord is my light and my salvation; whom shall I fear?* They delight in every kind of good work; their
Wis. 8:16 love of wisdom is such that *companionship with her has no bitterness, and life with her has no pain, but gladness and joy.* They set their minds on the things
Col. 3:1 above: *If then you have been raised with Christ, seek the things that are above, where Christ is.*[2] They see

[1] In Latin, the word for "wisdom" is *sapientia,* which Bonaventure connects with *sapida,* "tasteful," and *scientia,* "knowledge." Therefore he asserts that the term "wisdom" means "tasteful knowledge," i.e. the man of faith has an appetite for wise and doctrinally sound teaching.

[2] Bonaventure actually refers to Job 34:14 here, which in the Vulgate reads, "If he turns his heart to him, he shall draw his breath and spirit to himself." Modern scholarship has shown the Vulgate to be in error here, and so we have substituted a passage that better substantiates Bonaventure's point.

the baseness of worldly concerns: *I have seen every-*   *Eccles. 1:14*
thing that is done under the sun; and behold, all is
vanity and a striving after wind. And so they long most
for heaven: *My desire is to depart and to be with*   *Phil. 1:23*
Christ.

Love of God wipes out our sins and the punishment
due them: *Her sins, which are many, are forgiven for*   *Luke 7:47*
she loved much; but he who is forgiven little, loves
little. It increases the merit of our good deeds: *What is*   *Wis. 8:5*
richer than wisdom who effects all things? It helps us
build up our neighbor's faith: *Incense and a pleasing*   *Sir. 45:16*
odor as a memorial portion. We are the aroma of Christ   *2 Cor. 2:15*
to God.[3] Because we love God, demons flee from us:
Resist the devil and he will flee from you.[4] But the   *Jam. 4:7*
angels become our companions: *When you and your*   *Tob. 12:12*
daughter-in-law Sarah prayed, I (the angel Raphael is
speaking) . . . *was likewise present with you.*

3. The grace of devout love for God confers all these
benefits and many more, and so Christian leaders
should be especially eager to have it. Their love for
God will keep them always informed of what to do,
help them do it, and head them off from wrong directions. Heads must pray not for themselves alone, but
also for the people committed to their charge. They can
care for others properly only with divine help: *Unless*   *Ps. 127:1*
the Lord builds the house, those who build it labor in
vain.

The head of a community serves both God and those
whom he leads; he is a mediator between them. He
serves God by teaching God's people, correcting them,
and by all the good he does. He serves people by
pleading in prayer for their intentions and concerns
and for their protection from all harm: *I stood between*   *Deut. 5:5*

---

[3]Bonaventure imagines the virtues of a Christian as like odors
attractive enough to draw others to the Lord.

[4]Another substitution for the Vulgate. Bonaventure's original ref-
erence was Tobit 6:8, which in the Vulgate reads "The smoke thereof
driveth away all kinds of demons."

the Lord and you at that time.

4. We express devout love of God in three ways: public prayers in common with the whole community; private, personal prayer; and our constant awareness of God's presence in our daily lives.

Public Prayer

When the whole community worships God together, it should show devotion in its order, vigor and fervor. Every public religious service should be orderly and free from confusion, carelessness and delay, with each person fulfilling his responsibilities properly. *All things should be done decently and in order. David and the chiefs of the service also set apart for the service (those) . . . who should prophesy with lyres, with harps, and with cymbals.*

1 Cor. 14:40
1 Chron. 25:1

Since public worship is ministry to the Lord, we should take our part in it with vigor and a willing heart, not slothfully: *Cursed is he who does the work of the Lord with slackness.* The whole service should be conducted with devout reverence, giving full attention to each part. Prayers should be spoken or sung in a voice neither crashingly loud nor spiritlessly soft. After all, we are praying in the sight of the angels and in the presence of God: *Sing praise with all your heart and voice, and bless the name of the Lord.*

Jer. 48:10

Sir. 39:35

5. There are five reasons why the Spirit inspires the Christian people to celebrate public worship.

First, to imitate the heavenly choir, where saints and angels constantly sing God's praises in his very presence: *Blessed are those who dwell in thy house, ever singing thy praise.* According to Christ's own promise—*I am with you always, to the close of the age*—we have him truly present with us, both by his Spirit and in the Eucharist. He deserves all our honor and praise, and we ought to show him whatever rever-

Ps. 84:4

Matt. 28:20

ence we can. Unlike the singers in heaven, we cannot
maintain uninterrupted praise. But we can at least assist in worship to the fullest degree our weakness permits. By so giving ourselves to the praise of God, we
imitate the Jerusalem above, our mother.

    6. Second, we give thanks to God by offering prayers
and praise at specific times that commemorate his loving deeds on our behalf.[5] Christ was born of the Virgin
Mary at night; in the morning, before his passion, he
came before his judge. He also rose from the dead very
early in the morning. He was scourged at about nine in
the morning; this was also the hour at which he sent the
Holy Spirit upon the apostles. Noon was the hour of the
crucifixion; at three in the afternoon he died for us. In
the evening, at supper, he gave us the sacrament of his
body and blood.

    When we celebrate the mass, we commemorate the
Lord's passion. The mass also brings us the grace of his
presence, and under the form of the sacrament, provides the spiritual food of his body and blood. These
are things we should never forget, and so we commemorate them at specified times. *I will recount the
steadfast love of the Lord, the praises of the Lord,
according to all that the Lord has granted us.*

    7. Third, public worship stirs up our devotion and
fuels the fire of our love of God. Otherwise our idleness or the distraction of other activities will cause our
love to grow cold. The priests of the Old Testament
kept a fire constantly burning on the altar of the Temple, adding wood to it every morning. For us Christians, that fire is the fervor of devotion, which should
always burn on the altars of our hearts. Like the priest of
the Temple, a leader whose life is consecrated to God's
service should always nourish the fire of his love for
God by heaping on it the wood of the divine praises. *I*

Gal. 4:26

Isa. 63:7

Lev. 4:12-13

Ps. 34:1

---

[5]Bonaventure here refers to the official hours of prayer in the
monasteries.

will bless the Lord at all times; his praise shall con-
tinually be in my mouth.

8. Fourth, public worship is of special benefit to
immature or weak Christians who have trouble establishing a regular prayer life. When the whole community observes regular times of worship, these Christians
grow accustomed to a well-defined life of prayer. They
at least come to church to pray when the rest of the
community gathers there. Moreover, they will be more
likely to persevere in prayer if they can observe and
take part in the community celebration of the acts of
God. The liturgical services of the Jewish priesthood
Luke 1:10   had this function: *The whole multitude of the people*
were praying outside at the hour of incense.

The fact is that many poorly taught Christians hardly
ever spend time in personal prayer. It is all the more
important that they be called into church at definite
times to celebrate the saving acts of God and to hear the
word of God. Then they may develop the habit of
worship.

9. Fifth, even non-Christians and heretics gather together regularly for public worship. However mistaken
their beliefs, their faithfulness to worship should be an
example to us. We who know the truths of Christianity
have even greater reason to worship than they, so it is
fitting that our worship be orderly and beautiful. We
should come together both frequently and solemnly to
praise our Creator and to celebrate the true and holy
mysteries of our faith. Such worship brings us grace and
prepares us for eternal life. Services that are both solemn and fervent also attract ordinary Christians to a
Sir. 47:9-10   love and reverence for religious things. David *gave*
beauty to the feasts and arranged their times through-
out the year, while they praised God's holy name, and
the sanctuary resounded from early morning.

Of all the external observances of worship, we ought
to give the greatest attention to the official prayer of the

church,[6] conducting it in an orderly, vigorous and devout manner, as has been said before. At other times we are doing things for God, but here we stand before him, hearing and speaking to him; here we are able to beg him for help in our own necessities.

Private Prayer

10. Private prayer must also have a place in a Christian leader's life. He should be familiar with the psalms, litanies, and other vocal prayers so that he can recite them reflectively, choosing those that have the deepest meaning for him at a particular time. Our Savior recommended the Lord's Prayer as a vocal prayer: *When you pray, say "Our Father . . ."*

Luke 11:2; Matt. 6:9

A head should also spend time meditating on sacred things. He should bring before his mind's eye his own sins and shortcomings; he should reflect on future pains or on the benefits granted by God. He should consider Christ's passion, his goodness, and the rewards promised to his followers. Meditation on such subjects should lead to devout feelings of reverent love for God, of desire for him, and of sorrow for sin or joy in salvation. *I commune with my heart in the night; I meditate and search my spirit.*

Ps. 77:6

Feelings of personal attachment to God are of great importance. At times, one experiences tears or sighs or other indescribable movements of the heart: *the Spirit himself intercedes for us with sighs too deep for words.* One also feels a great sense of love, internal jubilations, intense rejoicing and rapture, and absorption of one's whole spirit in God: *He who is united to the Lord*

Rom. 8:26

1 Cor. 6:17

---

[6]Here Bonaventure refers to the public recitation of the Breviary, a prayer in the name of the whole Church that uses texts from Scripture, hymns, and lessons from the Fathers of the Church both to instruct those who recite the prayer and to praise God. It is still celebrated in the Catholic Church, and still consists largely of the psalms.

becomes one spirit with him. Such unity starts with a purification of our understanding that allows us to know God himself. That personal knowledge results in an ardent love for God which is so fulfilling that it binds us inseparably to him.

11. The leader's many responsibilities often distract him and get in the way of his devotional life. When that happens, he should at least take any brief opportunities he gets—as it were, secretly and by stealth—to restore himself to zealous prayer. No one should be so busy that he allows his fervor to grow completely cold, stops all prayer, drifts away from a personal relationship with God, and little by little abandons the grace given him, thus ceasing to please God. Moses, although taken up by duties to the people, often turned back to the Lord in the tent of the covenant. There he spoke personally with the Lord, finding in God refreshment for his spirit. Our Lord also, while preaching to the crowd by day, spent his nights in solitary prayer.

The head of a community may get few chances to spend a long time praying. But he is certainly given, at times, a greater grace of praying for others, since that is his duty. And it is right that those he is serving should have the benefit of his prayers. When he does have a chance to devote himself to prayer, he ought to make good use of it. He should try his best to find such chances, for if he ignores them, his ingratitude will deprive him of grace.

Awareness of God's Presence

12. The head, like anyone else who desires to grow spiritually by sharing his life with other Christians, ought to be constant in his devotion to God. Such constancy takes three forms.

First, the head should remain internally aware of God's yoke—the task and the grace that he has given to us. *I keep the Lord always before me. My eyes are ever toward the Lord.* Always and everywhere, a person should aim to live as if God were visibly present. So Elijah and Elisha used to say: *As the Lord of hosts lives, before whom I stand.* Such alertness requires that we turn our minds fully and decisively to the Lord.

The angels, wherever they may be sent, never stop gazing upon God; in the same way a virtuous person, as much as he can, always keeps the memory of God in his heart. If at times he fails in this, he should rebuke himself. Bernard of Clairvaux says, "Think of the time as lost when you have not been aware of God."⁷

Of course we cannot continually concentrate on the Lord in profound meditation; but at least we should remember his presence and direct the gaze of our hearts at him. When a sculptor obtains the material for a statue, he studies it from every angle; then, when an opportunity comes, he is ready to give it the proper shape. So too, mindfulness of God will be shaped into meditation or prayer when the opportunity comes.

13. The head should also maintain a constant determination to please God in every speech and action. This leads us to take as much care not to displease or grieve him as we would in his visible presence. Instead, we strive to make our deeds and our ways of doing things more pleasing to him: *Whether we are at home or away, we make it our aim to please him.*

A person who has committed himself to the Christian life should always act as though he were about to appear before the judgment seat of the Most High: *You also must be ready; for the Son of Man is coming at an hour you do not expect.* The Lord sees all of our actions; he does not forget our good deeds, but rewards them in due time. Neither will he neglect to punish our wrongdoing, if we do not do penance. *A man who breaks his*

Ps. 16:8; 25:15

1 Kings 18:15; see also 1 Kings 17:1 2 Kings 3:14

2 Cor. 5:9

Luke 12:40

Sir. 23:18-19

marriage vows says to himself, "Who sees me? Darkness surrounds me, and the walls hide me, and no one sees me. Why should I fear? The Most High will not take notice of my sins." His fear is confined to the eyes of men, and he does not realize that the eyes of the Lord are ten thousand times brighter than the sun; they look upon all the ways of men, and perceive even the hidden places.

14. Finally, a head should prepare for everything he does with prayer, at least mentally. Whatever the circumstances one can arm oneself with prayer and offer thanks and praise to God for all his goodness. A head asks the Lord to inspire him with worthwhile plans for his work, to direct his projects so that they help people reach salvation, and to preserve and increase the good done.

When a sailor can tell that a storm is coming, he usually makes haste to get to a safe port. In the same way, a committed Christian regularly turns to the harbor of prayer, where he can escape from all the conflicts that endanger him. In everything he has to do, he should put more confidence in prayer than in his own activity and labor: *O Our God, wilt thou not execute judgment upon them? For we are powerless against this great multitude that is coming against us. We do not know what to do, but our eyes are upon thee. As the eyes of servants look to the hand of their master, as the eyes of a maid to the hand of her mistress, so our eyes look to the Lord our God, till he have mercy on us.*

2 Chron. 20:12

Ps. 123:2

15. The spiritual head needs to have the qualities discussed above, and others as well, in order to do his service. The head is like one of the seraphim in Isaiah's vision whose six wings lift on high, cover their bodies and their feet, and rise above their heads. The character of a Christian leader is like the wings of the seraphim.

Isa. 6:1-4

First, the leader is raised up and sustained by a right intention and by brotherly love. Thus desire for human

praise will not infect his zeal, nor will personal prefer-
ences unbalance his compassion. The only reward he
seeks is in heaven: *I have inclined my heart to do thy*   Ps. 119:112
justifications forever; for the reward.

Next, patience and a life of good example protect him
from the spiritual spears of troublemakers and cover
the nakedness of lack of merits. These virtues are both
defensive armor and sacred vestments. *Put on your*   Isa. 52:1
strength, O Zion; put on your beautiful garments, O
Jerusalem, the holy city.

Prudent good judgment helps a leader, wherever he
goes, to see what he should do and how it should be
done. And by zealous devotion to God he seeks *the*   Col. 3:1
things that are above, where Christ is, seated at the
right hand of God, coming into his presence as though
he were borne aloft into that sublime height, his virtues
being like wings to raise him.

It is not possible for all spiritual leaders to possess all
these qualities equally. But it is absolutely necessary
that each leader possess at least some degree of each
virtue. This is just as important for the spiritual formation of those whom they direct as it is for their own
salvation.

Every Christian with a real commitment to God
ought to be adorned with these virtues; even if he has
only his own soul to govern, he will at the end come
before God's judgment seat to render an account for
that. These virtues, therefore, should lift him up like
wings and pinions: fervent righteousness, compassion
on his neighbors for the sake of God, patience in adversities, good example that helps others grow spiritually,
prudence in all things. Above all, every committed
Christian clings to God, maintaining his personal relationship with his Father through zealous prayer, asking
God to protect, direct and guide him in all things, and at
last to lead him up to heaven. May Jesus Christ merci-
fully grant this to us. Amen.

TRANSLATOR'S NOTE

The Latin text used in preparing this translation comes from the complete edition of Bonaventure's writings prepared by the Franciscan fathers of the College of St. Bonaventure (Quarracchi: 1898). In a few places, Bonaventure's references to Scripture have been changed to account for differences between the Vulgate and modern editions of the Bible. I have also modified Bonaventure's use of the analogy of the six-winged Seraph.

Our aim in publishing this translation is strictly pastoral. Consequently, we are not entering into the debate about Bonaventure's authorship of *De Sex Alis Seraphim,* which has been initiated by Rev. Ignatius Brady, O.F.M. in his article "The Writings of Saint Bonaventure Regarding the Franciscan Order," *Miscellanea Francescana* 1975.

In preparing this translation, I have occasionally benefited from study of two previous versions:

The Virtues of a Religious Superior, translated by Sabinus Mollitor, O.F.M. (St. Louis: 1920), and

The Six Wings of the Seraph, translated by Jose de Vinck in volume three of *The Works of Bonaventure: Cardinal, Seraphic Doctor, and Saint* (Paterson, New Jersey: 1966).

I am, however, responsible for any errors in this version.